COCKTAILS MADE SIMPLE

cocktails MADE SIMPLE

Easy & Delicious Recipes
for the Home Bartender

BRIAN WEBER & AMIN BENNY

Interior Photography by Biz Jones

ROCKRIDGE
PRESS

For general information on our other products and services or to obtain technical support, please contact our Customer Care Department within the United States at (866) 744-2665, or outside the United States at (510) 253-0500.

Rockridge Press publishes its books in a variety of electronic and print formats. Some content that appears in print may not be available in electronic books, and vice versa.

Interior and Cover Designer and Illustrations: Joshua Moore
Photo Art Director/Art Manager: Sara Feinstein
Editor: Sean Newcott
Production Editor: Edgar Doolan
Cover Photography: © Cameron Whitman/Stocksy
Interior Photography: © 2019 Biz Jones
Food Styling: Erika Joyce
Author Photo: © K Dulny and Alex Perkins Photography
Illustrations: © Colt Creative/Creative Market

ISBN: Print 978-1-64152-728-6 | eBook 978-1-64152-729-3

BRIAN

FOR MANDY, A KIND
AND GENEROUS SOUL,
AND ADAM, MY BUD,
WHO LEFT THIS WORLD
WAY TOO SOON

BENNY

TO THE LOVE OF MY LIFE,
MY BEAUTIFUL WIFE NICHOLE,
AND MY PRIDE AND JOY, MY
DAUGHTER SIMONE

Contents

PART II THE RECIPES 36

Introduction

It was the decade leading up to the millennium when film and television introduced drinks such as the Cosmopolitan (*Sex and the City*), the White Russian (*The Big Lebowski*), the Sidecar (*The Bonfire of the Vanities*), and the Margarita (*Practical Magic*). As people sipped on these popular concoctions with friends on a typical Saturday night, two bartenders in separate cities served crowds that were four or five people deep in line at the bar—shaking, stirring, and serving with a smile. That's us: Brian Weber in New York City and Amin Benny in Las Vegas. Little did we know that our shared passion for crafting cocktails and connecting with people would lead us to writing this book.

meet brian and benny

BRIAN After graduating from high school, I studied hospitality in Brooklyn while working full time in various restaurants. By 23, I was a head chef at a Manhattan brew pub, and later, a restaurant manager at a hotel. I went to Hawaii on vacation and ended up staying for five months, bartending to pay the bills. I returned to New York City and my love for music and sound production led to work at a recording studio. Then the 2008 financial crisis shuttered the studio. Undeterred, I launched my own audio company and returned to professional bartending at a wonderful private club. In 2013, I merged my passions for bartending and audio production; the *Bartender Journey* podcast was born and focused on bartender knowledge and information for both the professional bartender and the cocktail enthusiast.

BENNY I have had the honor of being a bartender for more than 21 years, so I like to say, "my bartending career can legally drink." My bartending career began the same way it ended, at high-end hotels; in that career I was lucky to work at some of the best hotels on the West Coast. I recently became a full-time ambassador for WhistlePig Rye Whiskey. As a bartender, my true passion lies in my cocktail creations and the guests with whom I get to share those creations. I believe that the guest at the bar should be treated like a guest at your home and you are their host, hence my trade name "The Bar Host."

a bartending basics book is born

As professional bartenders, we always look to improve our knowledge and skills. We had both joined the industry association, the United States Bartenders' Guild (USBG), and connected through USBG. Benny was already a fan of the *Bartender Journey* podcast, and working together to share our knowledge and passion just seemed right. We wanted to collaborate and write a cocktail book for beginners, because we're often approached by people looking for advice on how to bartend at home. Bartending books have become popular in recent years, but most books are written for professional bartenders and tackle advanced cocktails and concepts. This book will walk you through the basics and get you ready to become an amazing home bartender.

In the first part, we introduce you to the basics of bartending by beginning with terms and tools you should know. Then we cover essential ingredients and explain the techniques using those tools and ingredients to give you a foundation for creating cocktails. The second part of the book features recipes categorized by spirits. Each chapter starts with a brief description of the spirit and includes five classic cocktails that you'll be able to make using what you've learned from part I. Every recipe features a brief history of each cocktail, what you need to make the drink (glassware, tools, ingredients), and step-by-step instructions. We also give you tips and tricks along the way.

Our simple, straightforward approach will give you the knowledge to be confident. When it comes to making drinks, confidence is key, and the key to confidence is understanding and doing; we are going to make this simple, so you can understand and start doing. We are honored to be your guides on this bartender journey. Cheers!

PART I

The Art of Cocktails

Over the past 10 years, cocktail creation has become a true and respected craft. The same ingredients that are used within the kitchen have moved over to the bar, and bartenders are slowly climbing up to the heights of some of the top chefs. This, in turn, has given rise to an individual known as the "cocktail enthusiast," an educated consumer who is sometimes more informed and precise than many longtime bartenders!

Cocktail enthusiasts helped create the demand for cocktails as culinary concoctions, containing fresh ingredients and quality spirits. This current, sophisticated approach also comes with a degree of respect for the long history of bartending.

Cocktail enthusiasts have also set home bartending on the rise and have emerged themselves as an essential part of the new cocktail culture. Together, professional bartenders and consumers are building this culture up and creating a community based on strong relationships, shared knowledge, and the highest level of hospitality that is shared with anyone who has a love for cocktails.

1

The Terms

Learning the language will help you understand the world of cocktails. Here are terms you should know before moving forward with this book that will get you speaking like a pro.

ALCOHOL BY VOLUME ("ABV"): Tells you the percentage of alcohol in the bottle.

APÉRITIF: A spirit meant to awaken the appetite due to its slightly bitter flavor, which causes salivation.

AROMATIZED WINES: Wines that have been infused with herbs and spices. Vermouths fall within this category.

BALANCE: A term used to describe all the components of a cocktail working together in perfect proportion. This is what you strive to achieve when creating cocktails.

BASE SPIRIT: The main spirit or liquor used in the cocktail. Examples include vodka, gin, rum, tequila, whisk(e)y, or brandy.

BATCHING: Creating multiple cocktails at one time for a large group so that they are fully or partially prepared before guests arrive. The point is to speed up the cocktail-making process when hosting a crowd.

BUILD: Adding one ingredient at a time into the glass with no other preparation required. Also describes how you add your ingredients to the shaker tin or mixing glass. This is a great way for a beginner to start creating cocktails with fewer tools.

COCKTAIL: In 1806, *The Balance and Columbian Repository* described a cocktail as "spirits of any kind, sugar, water, and bitters," but in today's world we tend to call all alcoholic mixed drinks "cocktails."

COCKTAIL ENTHUSIAST: A die-hard cocktail fan who is not a professional bartender or in the industry.

DASH: A measurement commonly used for adding bitters to cocktails. Bitters bottles usually come with a dasher cap, so adding a dash is easy. There are approximately 8 dashes in 1 teaspoon.

DIGESTIF: A spirit that aids in the digestion of food and therefore consumed after a meal.

DILUTION: When water is added to a cocktail, usually through ice melting during shaking or stirring. Dilution is important in the cocktail-making process and accounts for 20–25 percent of many drinks; however, with more dilution than that, the balance of your ingredients is thrown out of proportion.

DISCARD: To throw out after use or to reject as a whole. This is usually done when a drink is messed up or a guest is done drinking it.

DRESSED: When the cocktail has a rim, garnish, or other elements added for presentation purposes. If nothing is added for presentation, it is generally called "undressed."

FILLER: A nonalcoholic ingredient in the cocktail, such as juice or soda.

FORTIFIED: This is when a little alcohol is added to something, such as in fortified wines or in solutions that are used to preserve something for a longer period of time.

GARNISH: The addition of an ingredient to your cocktail that may or may not add to the taste of the drink. It's often fruit but could really be almost anything.

LIQUEUR: A sweetened, flavored spirit. Liqueurs fall within the "modifier" portion of the cocktail, unless it is the base spirit of the drink, such as the recipes in chapter 12.

MODIFIER: Describes liqueurs, vermouths, or alcoholic ingredients in the cocktail that do not fall into the category of base spirits.

NEAT: The spirit in the glass without anything else.

ON THE ROCKS: The spirit in the glass with only ice added. (Ice cubes are called rocks.)

PART: This describes a proportion without using an exact measurement. For example, the cocktail is two parts spirit and one part vermouth. These proportions would be the same whether you are creating one cocktail or batching fifty.

RINSE: Washing the inside of a glass with an aromatic spirit and then discarding the remaining spirit. This is used to create a subtle hint of flavor and aroma.

ROLL: Pouring the cocktail from one tin or glass to another to mix the cocktail. This technique is useful for when the cocktail is too large to fit in the sealed tin but will fit in the tin unsealed.

SHAKE: Creating a cocktail in a shaker tin set, adding ice and shaking the drink. Shaking the cocktail is a common technique and probably one of the most fun, because you can really add your own style and movements.

SPENT ICE: The ice that was used in the cocktail-making process during shaking or stirring. This ice should be discarded after using and fresh ice should be used if the drink is to be served on the rocks.

SPIRIT: Another word for liquor. It gains this name because in the distillation process it is evaporated and turned back into liquid to create alcohol.

STIR: Gently rotating the cocktail and ice in a mixing glass using a long bar spoon. Stirring is one of the most common techniques to create cocktails.

STRAIGHT UP: A cocktail that is served without ice.

TRANSPARENT: Ingredients that you are able to see through.

TWIST/ZEST/PEEL: The skin or rind of a citrus fruit that holds the essential oils, usually cut using a peeler. The peel is often used as a garnish to add a layer of flavor.

COCKTAIL CONSTRUCTION

1. When you construct a cocktail, begin with the nonalcoholic ingredients because they are the cheapest. If you make a mistake and need to discard your mixture, it won't include expensive ingredients like booze. The only exception to this is carbonated beverages: hold them until after shaking to avoid a messy explosion!
2. Add modifiers next because, although costly, you usually need very little.
3. Then add your base spirits and add ice last because you want to control your cocktail's dilution.
4. When your cocktail is prepared, strain into an empty glass and add ice, if required. Don't put the ice in first because you may not be able to fit the entire cocktail in the glass.

2

The Tools

In the art of building cocktails, there is an array of tools to help you create your desired concoctions. This chapter describes the tools needed to make the cocktails in this book and helps you assemble a tool collection for your home bar. Now, let's take your first steps on your journey to a better cocktail.

tools of the trade

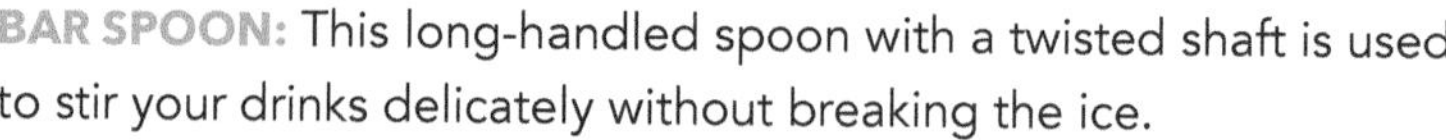

BAR SPOON: This long-handled spoon with a twisted shaft is used to stir your drinks delicately without breaking the ice.

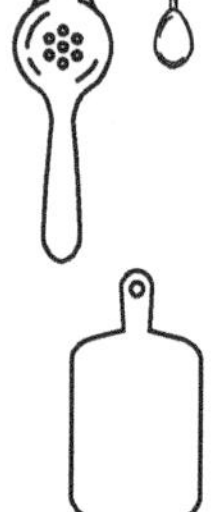

CITRUS SQUEEZER: Used to squeeze the juice out of citrus fruit to create fresh fruit juice. A handheld citrus squeezer is affordable, portable, and good for small amounts of citrus.

CUTTING BOARD: Made of wood or plastic and is the surface used to cut your garnishes.

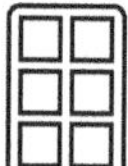

ICE TRAY: While these come in many styles and sizes, you need at least one to make large cubes for cocktails that call for a single "rock" (slang for ice cube).

JIGGER: Measures exact amounts of liquids for you to pour for your cocktail. Our favorite is the Japanese jigger; its tall and thin design controls spillage.

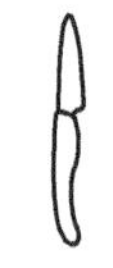

KNIFE: Best for cutting garnishes. We recommend a knife with a 3-inch serrated blade.

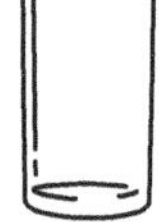

MIXING GLASS: A glass that is heavy in weight so it is stabilized while in use; used for cocktails that need to be stirred.

MUDDLER: Helps mash or press solids (e.g., herbs, fruits, or spices) to release flavors. It is usually made of wood, plastic, or stainless steel and has a rigid bottom. We prefer the flat-bottom muddlers because they work best with herbs and fruit.

PEELER: Separates the zest (the skin) from the pith (white part) of the citrus fruit. (The pith of fruits is not used due to the bitter taste.)

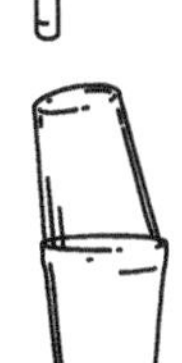

SHAKER: Shakers are used to mix up your cocktails and come in an array of types and styles. A Boston shaker set is two shakers that connect and lock, which helps prevent spillage. (Sets that are glass-on-tin are hard to handle during shaking and do not chill as well.) The Cobbler shaker is a three-piece shaker set consisting of a shaker tin, a top with a built-in strainer, and a lid that you remove after shaking to pour your cocktail into the glass. You will not need a strainer for this shaker, but the top is sometimes hard to get off when it is cold.

STRAINER: A metal tool that allows you to pour the mixed drink by separating it from the ice. A Hawthorne strainer has a spring and is generally used when straining from a mixing tin. A julep strainer is a round, bowl-shaped strainer that fits tightly over a mixing glass. It is generally used when straining from a mixing glass. A mesh or fine strainer is used when adding solids to your shaker, like fruit, vegetables, herbs, or purée, to remove any small debris or ice shards that may get through on a single strain.

WORK WITH WHAT YOU HAVE

The tools you use are important in the process and final cocktail, but if you don't have every tool available, here are a few MacGyver-like tips and substitutions to help get you started on your bartending journey.

IF YOU DON'T HAVE A SHAKER: Use two plastic cups that fit into each other for mixing and instead of shaking your drink, you can "roll" it, pouring from one cup to the other until it is mixed. Important note: The cups should be plastic to avoid breakage.

IF YOU DON'T HAVE A STRAINER: To strain out the spent ice, put an empty cup into the cup containing the cocktail, just enough to hold back the ice but still let you pour out the finished cocktail. Note that the bottom of the cup is touching your drink, so it must always be clean.

IF YOU DON'T HAVE A BAR SPOON: For stirred drinks, build the cocktail in one glass and use an item with considerable length, such as chopsticks, as a stand-in bar spoon. Then use the strainer method outlined above to separate the cocktail from the spent ice.

Some great brands and places to find bar tools: CocktailKingdom.com for top-quality tools; ABarAbove.com shop, which sells Top Shelf Bar Supply; and the XOX brands that you can find in many stores.

the glassware

Glassware is the vessel that holds and showcases your cocktail, so it should be both functional and visually pleasing. What you use is determined by how it is served, the size of the drink, and the "presentation" you want for your cocktail. This section will help you understand why certain cocktails require certain glassware and get you one step closer to mastering home bartending.

CHAMPAGNE FLUTE: The flute is used to hold sparkling wines or sparkling cocktails. The tall, narrow bowl provides minimal exposure to air, so fewer bubbles escape.

Used for: French 75, Bellini, Mimosa

COCKTAIL COFFEE GLASS: Also known as an irish coffee glass, this is a clear, mug-style glass with a base and a handle to keep the heat off your hands. Perfect for any hot cocktail.

Used for: Irish Coffee, Hot Toddy, Blue Blazer

COCKTAIL GLASS: Two popular types that fall into this category are the martini glass and the coupe glass. A martini glass is named after the cocktail that is meant to go inside of it. It has a V-shape, a stem, and a base. A coupe glass is a shallow bowl-shaped glass rumored to be shaped after Marie Antoinette's left breast so that her court could toast to her health. Both are for cocktails that are meant to be "straight up" (i.e., without ice).

Used for: Martini, Manhattan, Cosmopolitan

COLLINS/HIGHBALL GLASS: The Collins and the Highball glasses are both used for tall drinks that usually have ice in them. They are named after the cocktails that are meant to go inside them but can be used for any tall cocktail. These glasses are both round and tall with a flat base and hold 8 to 12 ounces of fluid, so they can be used to serve sodas as well.

Used for: Tom Collins, Gin and Tonic, Mojito

ROCKS/OLD FASHIONED GLASS: The rocks or old fashioned glass is meant for short cocktails that are to be served on the rocks (with ice) or neat (spirit only). The difference between the two is that the rocks glass is plain in design and the old fashioned glass is often made of a thick, etched glass meant to have a better look and hand feel.

Used for: Old Fashioned, Margarita, Moscow Mule

WINE GLASS: The wine glass is mostly used for drinking wine but sometimes for cocktails as well. Cocktails that have wine in them will usually be put in a wine glass. The wine glass has a large bowl on top with a stem and a flat base to hold it up.

Used for: Aperol Spritz

If you're stocking your home bar for the first time, we recommend investing in classic cocktail glasses first because they are used most often and working up to investing in more specialty glassware if you so choose.

After reading this you can begin to understand that all glassware has functioning parts that cater to that style of cocktail. Cocktail and champagne glasses have stems because the cocktails within do not have ice; you hold the stems so your body heat does not warm the cocktail. Drinks in tall and short glasses will usually have ice, so your body heat will not greatly affect the cocktail. And hot cocktails go in a glass with a handle so you can comfortably pick up the hot drink. As you perfect your cocktail creations, you will find more types of glassware that you can use to show off your style, but the glasses listed above are the basics that will get you started.

WORK WITH WHAT YOU HAVE

Don't stress if you don't have a specific glass; you can always use alternative glasses that you have at home, because the true purpose is to get you started on your cocktail creation adventures. For straight-up cocktails (i.e., served without ice), any stemware around the house will work, even a wine glass, as long as the cocktail fits inside. Highball, Collins, and rocks glasses are among the most common in a typical kitchen. A trick you can use is to add the ice last; if the cocktail takes up too much room, the glass will get less ice, but you never want to waste any of the cocktail. Hot cocktails can go in coffee mugs, since the most important factor is to ensure the drinker doesn't get burned by a hot glass. As you grow your home bartending skills, you can decide how you want your glassware collection to grow, but never feel you cannot work with what you have.

3

The Ingredients

In this chapter we will explore the necessary ingredients to help you build amazing cocktails at home without breaking your budget. Your personal taste determines how you build your home bar, so begin with your favorite spirits. The examples list our recommended brands, and some may be familiar to you. Let's walk you through all the ingredients that will be the stars of your cocktail show; it will be as simple as syrup!

liquors

When we think of liquor, we think of any alcoholic drink that's typically been distilled and can be enjoyed as is (neat) or served as the base in a mixed drink. There are many different varieties and it all comes down to personal taste, but understanding the different varieties of liquors available is essential to building a practical and functional home bar. Unless otherwise indicated, these liquors can be made anywhere in the world.

BRANDY: A spirit distilled from different fruits, most commonly grapes. Popular categories include Cognac, pisco, and Calvados. When a recipe calls for brandy without specifying a category, it is referring to a brandy distilled from grapes.

Examples: *Copper & Kings (American brandy), Pierre Ferrand (Cognac), Campo de Encanto (pisco)*

GIN: A neutral spirit produced using a variety of botanicals (spices, herbs, fruits, and more), with additional botanical flavors added. Traditionally, the most prominent flavor is juniper, but there is a wide variety of creative gins available. It could be said that gin is a "flavored vodka." There are three main categories with different flavor profiles: Old Tom, London Dry, and Modern Gin. Gin can be made anywhere in the world.

Examples of Old Tom: *Queen's Courage, Ransom*

Examples of London Dry: *Bombay, Fords*

Examples of Modern Gin: *Hendrick's, Nolet's*

RUM: A sugar-based spirit available in many different styles with very few rules on how it can be made, which makes rum one of the most diverse spirits.

Examples: *Bacardi, Plantation, Appleton*

TEQUILA: An agave-based spirit that is unique to Mexico. The best quality tequilas are made from 100 percent agave from the Blue Weber species. An agave is a flowering plant that looks like a cactus but is more closely related to asparagus.

Examples: *Patrón, Azuñia, Fortaleza*

VODKA: A neutral spirit that is colorless and odorless and has no dominant flavor. It can be made from grain, potatoes, or fruits, and may be produced anywhere in the world.

Examples: *Ketel One, Tito's, St. George*

WHISK(E)Y: A grain-based (think barley, corn, wheat, rye, etc.) spirit that is almost always aged in barrels. Think of whisk(e)y as a tree that has many different but related branches of flavor. Below are a few of these branches:

BOURBON WHISKEY: Primarily a corn-based spirit that is aged; can be made anywhere in America.

Examples: Buffalo Trace, Wild Turkey, Bulleit

RYE WHISKEY: Mostly made of rye and can be made anywhere in the world.

Examples: WhistlePig, Old Overholt, Sazerac

SCOTCH WHISKY: This type of whisky falls into two categories: single malt (made at one distillery) or blended (made up of whiskies from multiple distilleries). Scotch is a barley-based spirit that is aged and can only be made in Scotland.

Examples of single malt: The Macallan, Glenmorangie

Examples of blended: Johnnie Walker, Monkey Shoulder

Other categories include **Canadian Whisky** *(usually blended whisky),* **Irish Whiskey** *(mostly barley-based), and* **Japanese Whisky***, which is becoming as popular as Scotch Whisky. (As you can see, some countries use an "e" and others do not in spelling whisk[e]y.)*

liqueurs / apéritifs / digestifs

A **liqueur** is a sweetened, flavored spirit. An **apéritif** is a spirit meant to awaken the appetite with its slightly bitter flavor, which causes you to salivate. A **digestif** is a spirit that aids in the digestion of food. These can all be enjoyed neat, but when added to cocktails, they are known as modifiers.

AMARETTO: A traditional Italian liqueur usually made from almonds or apricot pits.

APEROL: A light and bitter Italian apéritif that is flavored predominantly with orange, herbs, and roots.

CAMPARI: A very bitter Italian apéritif that is flavored with herbs, plants, and fruit.

COINTREAU: An orange-flavored French liqueur that falls within the triple sec category but has a higher alcohol content than many other liqueurs.

CRÈME DE CASSIS: A liqueur that has a high sugar content, made from the flavor of black currants.

FERNET-BRANCA: A bitter Italian digestif that is flavored with herbs and spices.

PIMM'S NO. 1: A gin-based liqueur that is flavored with herbs, oranges, and spices.

fortified wines / aromatized wines / sparkling wines

Fortified wines have small amounts of additional alcohol added. Aromatized wines have botanicals added.

DRY VERMOUTH: A white aromatic wine that is also known as "French vermouth" (but can be made anywhere) or "white vermouth," and is dry in flavor.

Example: *Noilly Prat*

SPARKLING WINE: A carbonated wine that is usually white or rosé. For cocktails, these are sometimes called "bubbles" and used in a variety of sparkling cocktails.

Examples: *champagne, prosecco*

SWEET VERMOUTH: This is a red aromatic wine that is also known as "Italian vermouth" (but also can be made anywhere in the world) or "red vermouth," and is sweet in flavor.

Example: *Martini & Rossi*

Both dry and sweet vermouths are usually fortified.

mixers

Mixers can add flavor and/or carbonation to help create a balanced cocktail.

CITRUS: Meaning lime juice or lemon juice, citrus is one of the most important filler ingredients in the cocktail-making process and is usually leveled out with syrup to create balance within the cocktail. Freshly squeezed juice tastes better, thus creating a better cocktail. Always remove excess pulp from freshly squeezed juice by using a mesh strainer, to create visually pleasing cocktails. Even though orange and grapefruit juice are citrus and taste better when freshly squeezed, they do not fall into the citrus-syrup balance spectrum, because they are not bitter enough.

JUICES: Used in cocktails and are usually made from fruit, either freshly squeezed or packaged. The higher-quality juice you use, the better drink you will make.

> ***Examples:*** *lemon, lime, orange, grapefruit, tomato*

SODA: A carbonated water that can have syrups added for flavor and sweetness.

> ***Examples:*** *soda water (club soda, seltzer water), tonic water, ginger ale, ginger beer, cola*

SYRUP: A sweetener typically made from sugar dissolved in water. It is so simple that one recipe is called simple syrup. Syrup will usually be one part sugar and one part water, but you can change your recipes using different sweeteners in the same proportion. Demerara sugar makes the best simple syrup, but you may also use refined sugar, brown sugar, honey, agave nectar, maple syrup, or molasses to make different and interesting syrups.

> ***Examples:*** *grenadine, which is equal parts pomegranate juice and sugar*

CLASSY CLASSIFICATIONS

Here are the six most popular "cocktail families."

Classic Cocktail: spirit, sugar, bitters
Example: Old Fashioned

Collins: spirit, citrus, sugar, soda or sparkling wine
Example: Tom Collins, Mojito

Daisy: spirit, liqueur, citrus, sugar
Example: Margarita, Sidecar

Fizz: spirit, citrus, sugar, soda, egg whites
Example: Sloe Gin Fizz, Ramos Gin Fizz

Highball: spirit, soda
Example: Gin and Tonic

Sour: spirit, citrus, sugar (egg whites optional)
Example: Whiskey Sour, Daiquiri, Bee's Knees

garnishes and flavorings

Garnishes are broken down into three categories: functional, nonfunctional, and nonedible. Functional garnishes are used to complement the cocktail and add flavor. Examples include a lime wedge, an orange twist (or "peel"), or a salt-rimmed glass. Nonfunctional garnishes are for appearances only and do not add anything to the cocktail. Examples are a lime wheel (slice), a pineapple leaf, or an edible flower. Nonedible garnishes accompany the cocktail and are not meant to be eaten. Examples are a paper umbrella, a glowing ice cube, or a swizzle stick.

ANGOSTURA AROMATIC BITTERS: A popular type and brand of bitters that appears in many recipes. Bitters add a level of flavor to cocktails.

CHERRY (MARASCHINO): Used as an edible garnish. For best flavor, avoid the bright red ones and buy Luxardo (made with sour Marasca cherries and preserved in its liqueur).

GRAPEFRUIT: Used to make wedges, wheels, halfwheels, and peels. The sour to semisweet and somewhat bitter citrus flavor of the juice can also be used to flavor cocktails.

LEMON: Used to make wedges, wheels, halfwheels, and peels.

LIME: Used to make wedges, wheels, halfwheels, and peels.

MINT: Used as an edible garnish to add aroma to the cocktail. For the best flavor, buy fresh mint with a vibrant green color. Muddled mint leaves are also used to infuse a cocktail with the herb's flavor and aroma.

If you purchase or pick mint, keep it fresh by cutting the bottoms of the stems and plunging them into a bowl of very cold ice water. After about 15 minutes, let it drip dry in a colander. While still slightly moist, wrap the mint in paper towels and put into a resealable plastic bag. Store in the refrigerator for about five days.

OLIVES: Used as an edible garnish. Olives can be dropped directly into the cocktail or skewered and placed in or across the rim of the glass. They come in a variety of flavors, from plain to stuffed with other savory ingredients.

ORANGES: Used to make wheels, halfwheels, and peels.

SALT: It is best to use sea salt. This is commonly used on the rim of the glass and sometimes in the cocktail itself.

SUGAR: Sugar can also go on the rim of the glass or inside the cocktail when called for in a recipe.

THE IMPORTANCE OF ICE

You may not give it much thought, but ice is a major contributor to your cocktail. Ice keeps the cocktail cold, but it also provides dilution, which creates balance. Dilution (ice melting into the cocktail) also means that water quality is important because it becomes part of your drink, so you may want to consider using filtered water to make ice for cocktails. Types of ice include large cubes, cracked ice, and crushed ice. You can make ice at home with trays or buy it at your local grocery store or online (IceBulb.com sells luxury ice). Smaller pieces of ice melt more quickly than large pieces, which leads to faster dilution.

The Techniques

In the case of cocktails, the technique is the process used to make your cocktail, such as stirring for spirit-forward flavors, or shaking for cocktails with citrus. We are going to break down each technique for you, so you can understand the best methods for creating balanced cocktails.

shake things up

BUILDING: This is simply making a drink directly in the glass in which it will be served.

DOUBLE SHAKING/DRY SHAKING: When you shake your cocktail twice—once with ice and once without—the portion without ice is called "dry shaking," and the whole process is called "double shaking" (not to be confused with shaking two cocktails at once). This prevents overdiluting cocktails that call for an extra-long shake (usually cocktails with egg or cream). This technique adds a rich texture to your cocktails and creates a foamy head on top of the drink.

DOUBLE STRAINING: Anytime you add solids when building a cocktail, it is best practice to double strain. When a recipe instructs you to muddle or shake herbs, you will get tiny pieces in your cocktail that neither of the traditional strainers can completely eliminate on its own. First use either a Hawthorne or julep strainer followed by a mesh strainer on the cocktail.

EXPRESSING OILS: A fruit peel's essential oils can add a layer of flavor and aroma to your cocktail. With a peeler or small knife, take a zest from the citrus fruit (roughly 2 to 3 inches long and about ¾ inch wide). Holding it between your index fingers and thumbs of both hands, gently fold the peel to express the oils from the skin over the drink.

FLAMING A CITRUS PEEL: A technique using the essences from the peel and fire to create a spray of flame. This works because the oils in the peel are flammable. By holding the peel by its edges next to a flame and gently squeezing the peel, the oils will be released, and this will create a spray of fire directed over the cocktail. This technique is a showstopper and will definitely impress your guests, but understand that anytime you play with fire, you must always use extreme caution.

finishing touches

CITRUS TWIST/SPIRAL/PEEL: Use a y-peeler or spiral peeler to create a twist and a channel knife to make spirals on citrus fruit. A twist or zest is used to express the peel's essential oils from the skin into the drink. A spiral is a nonfunctional garnish that is mostly used for decoration.

FLOATING HERBS: By putting a single herb on top of your cocktail, you are "floating" the herb. This looks best on cocktails that are served straight up; it allows the herb to float on the cocktail like a boat in a lake.

GARNISH A GLASS WITH CITRUS: Some cocktails will call for a citrus wedge or wheel to sit on the rim of the glass. Wedges can also be added to the drink for added flavor. When preparing your citrus garnishes, always put a cut in the garnish so that you can easily set it on the rim if you wish.

MUDDLING: You will need a muddler for this, and there are two ways of muddling: Use a gentle press when you are dealing with herbs, but completely smash whole fruits.

RIMMING A GLASS: You can add any ground spice to the rim of a glass to add another layer of flavor to the cocktail, but sugar and salt are the most common choices. The rim should be on the outside of the glass so that it does not mix into your drink. Place spice, sugar, or salt on a flat plate and rub a citrus wedge on the area of the glass where you want the spice to stick. Roll the outside of the glass on the plate, so that the solids adhere to the outside of the glass. Pro Tip: Dress only half the rim to give the drinker the option to indulge in more or less of the spice, sugar, or salt.

RINSING: The point of rinsing is to get the smell of the spirit into your drink without needing to add the spirit itself to the mixed cocktail. You will achieve this by adding a small amount of a spirit to the empty cocktail glass, rolling it around, and then discarding the remaining spirit before pouring the finished drink into the rinsed glass.

SHAKING: Shaking will chill, dilute, mix, and add texture to your cocktail. Hold the secured shaker tin with both hands, dominant hand on top and one hand on each piece, and aim away from your guests. You will shake the cocktail back and forth in a steady side-to-side motion between shoulder and head level for about 10 seconds. This is your time to shine, and some people who really get into their shake even create a dance. Shaking is commonly used for cocktails that have citrus, cream, egg, or other ingredients that are not transparent.

SPANKING HERBS: This technique is used to awaken an herb, releasing the essential oils so that it will become more aromatic. Place the herb in the palm of one hand and clap on it with your other hand. Alternatively, you can grasp the herbs in one hand and lightly slap a sprig of herbs against the opposite wrist. Remember, you don't solely taste with your mouth, but also with your nose.

STIRRING: For this process you will need a mixing glass and a bar spoon. This is a very gentle technique and is used for spirit-forward cocktails. The key to this is to not mix or break the ice, but to move the ice as a unit by always having the rounded side of the spoon touching the inside of the mixing glass. Each stir is a "rotation." Put the bar spoon between your middle and ring finger, pinching it with your index and thumb, then stir by using your fingers only—the proper execution of this doesn't involve moving your wrist. This process gets easier with practice, so make lots of cocktails and you will improve over time.

STRAINING: This is when you use a strainer to separate the liquid from the ice in a shaker or mixing glass. Straining is done even if the drink is served over ice. The best practice is to use fresh ice in the glass instead of the spent ice used to create the cocktail.

Now that you know the terms, tools, ingredients, and techniques, you are ready to start making wonderful cocktails at home. As a home bartender, you can have fun not only drinking cocktails but also making them!

PART II

The Recipes

Cocktails are a social, satisfying experience. Making something for friends and family that is delicious and brings a smile to their faces is a real thrill. With these recipes, you will learn to "craft" a great drink using quality ingredients and essential technqiues.

In the culinary world there are "mother sauces" upon which countless variations can be created. Classic cocktails are like the "mother sauces" of the beverage world; fabulous on their own and capable of endless variations that you can play with to craft your own original creations!

In this section, we will present the recipes by category of base spirit, so that you can quickly jump to your favorite, but we encourage you to explore spirits that you don't often drink. These recipes are a great jumping-off point to broaden your horizons. It is our sincere hope that you will continue your cocktail journey and education beyond this book.

Keep in mind that while we have provided examples of different spirits, you generally do not need to use a specific brand for a recipe (except where a product is unique); there are countless exciting products on the market.

You should always give your drink a little taste before serving it to guests. We do our best to be very specific about measurements and ingredients, but variations do occur naturally. Even small errors in measurement can make a large difference.

Please note, each recipe yields one drink unless otherwise noted, and when "chilled" glassware is called for, be sure to place the glass in the freezer for at least five minutes before pouring the cocktail in.

Now, let's make some cocktails. Cheers!

Bee's Knees,
page 48

5

Gin

Gin is experiencing a boom in popularity, and for good reason—it is a versatile and delicious spirit. It is produced by redistilling a high-proof alcohol with botanicals. Juniper is the prominent flavor to expect in gin, but everything from citrus and cinnamon to various spices and roots are used.

There are several categories of gin, including Old Tom, Plymouth, and Modern, but we will stick to London Dry gin for our purposes. Not only is it the most recognizable category but also the original London Dry gin requirements were created to ensure the highest quality, including requiring all flavors to be natural (i.e., no synthetic additions) and mandating that the only additives after distillation can be water and 0.01g of sugar per liter of alcohol.

gin and tonic

GLASSWARE & TOOLS

12-ounce Highball glass

Jigger

Bar spoon

A gin and tonic is a perfect Highball-style drink for a warm summer day, or any day when you are in the mood for a classic, refreshing cocktail. You may be surprised to learn that the history behind this drink involves a literal life-and-death situation. In the early nineteenth century, the army of the British East India Company discovered that quinine could prevent malaria, but the taste was bitter and unpalatable. The soldiers mixed it with water, gin, sugar, and lime, and the rest is history. To quote Winston Churchill, "The gin and tonic has saved more Englishmen's lives than all the doctors in the Empire."

INGREDIENTS & METHOD

Fill the glass with as much ice as possible. **Add** the gin. **Pour** in the tonic water until the glass is full. **Stir** gently to combine the ingredients–two or three rotations should be enough. **Garnish** with a lime wedge.

There are many affordable craft tonics on the market, so no need to settle for the supermarket brand if you'd like to experiment.

TIP The lime wedge should be perched on the side of the glass, so that the drinker can squeeze it into the drink. To accomplish this, make a cut in the middle of the lime wedge, halfway through the fruit.

tom collins

GLASSWARE & TOOLS

12-ounce Collins glass (or 12-ounce Highball glass)

Citrus juicer

Jigger

Shaker

Strainer

Bar spoon

This is a delicious drink whose flavor profile suffered for many years from being made with artificial sour mix from soda guns at bars. When made with fresh lemon juice and simple syrup, this is a wonderful, refreshing, and impressive cocktail. A note on the glassware: As the name implies, a Collins glass is ideal for this drink: it is similar to a Highball glass, only a bit skinnier and a bit taller. It's up to you if you want to splurge on both Highball and Collins glassware, but a Highball glass will work just fine.

INGREDIENTS & METHOD

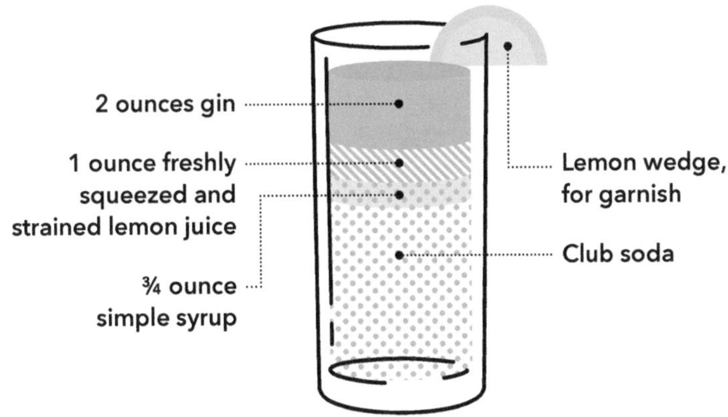

Add the gin, lemon juice, and simple syrup to the shaker. **Add** ice and shake until very cold, about 15 seconds. **Fill** the glass with as much ice as possible. **Strain** the contents of the shaker into the ice-filled glass. **Top** with club soda. **Stir** gently to combine–three rotations should be enough. **Garnish** with a lemon wedge.

Learning to make this drink is a jumping-off point for endless variations. Muddle some strawberries, add some herbs, and/or change the base spirit to create your own original cocktail.

negroni

GLASSWARE & TOOLS

- Old fashioned glass
- Mixing glass
- Jigger
- Bar spoon
- Peeler

Like most things bar-related, the history of the Negroni is a little fuzzy. Most accounts trace the beginnings of this cocktail to Florence, Italy, around 1919. The story goes that Count Camillo Negroni enjoyed drinking Americanos at Caffè Casoni. He asked the bartender to make his favorite drink stronger, and the bartender replaced the sparkling water with gin. This is what we refer to as an "equal parts cocktail" for obvious reasons. A favorite of bartenders and cocktail aficionados, the Negroni is somewhat of an acquired taste, but once you acquire it, you may find yourself craving them.

INGREDIENTS & METHOD

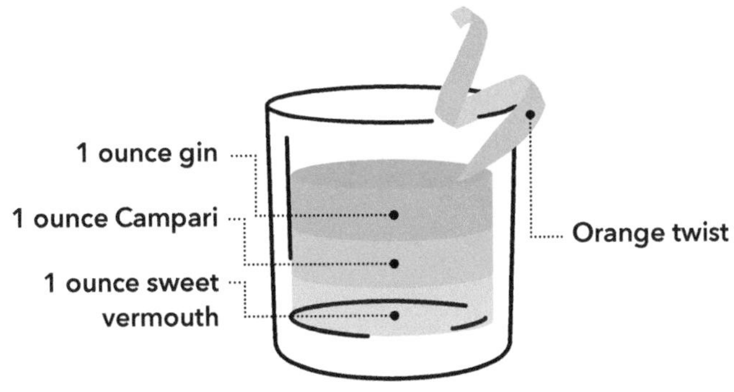

Pour all the liquid ingredients into a mixing glass with ice. **Stir** until very cold, about 15 seconds. **Strain** into the old fashioned glass with one large ice cube. **Express** the oils from the orange twist, rub onto the rim, and place in the drink.

martini

GLASSWARE & TOOLS

Martini glass, coupe glass, or cocktail glass (chilled)

Mixing glass

Bar spoon

Strainer

Professional bartenders like to say, "A Martini is not a cocktail, it's a conversation." Most Martini drinkers know exactly how they like their drink made; anything else just isn't right. A classic Martini is made with gin, though some people prefer vodka. The next ingredient is dry vermouth, and the proper amount is often debated. In the early twentieth century, 2:1 gin to vermouth was the norm, but that has steadily decreased over the years and some people don't want vermouth at all. This recipe uses a 4:1 ratio, and you can feel free to adjust to taste.

INGREDIENTS & METHOD

Put the bitters (if using), vermouth, and gin in a mixing glass with ice. **Stir** until very cold, about 15 seconds. **Strain** into the chilled glass. If using olives, put them on a cocktail pick and in the glass before straining the drink. Always use an odd number of olives—an even number is bad luck. If adding a twist, strain the drink into the glass, then hold the twist lengthwise just over the glass in the thumb and index finger of each hand and gently fold to express the oils from the peel. **Rub** the twist on the rim of the glass. **Put** the twist in the drink.

Shaken or stirred?
We like to say James Bond ordered his Martini "shaken not stirred," but that's the exception to the rule. That's fine for Mr. Bond, but a Martini is traditionally stirred, creating a silky texture with no air bubbles.

bee's knees

GLASSWARE & TOOLS

Martini glass, coupe glass, or cocktail glass (chilled)

Citrus juicer

Shaker

Jigger

Strainer

Another Prohibition-era cocktail, the Bee's Knees is quite delicious. The expression "the bee's knees" means being the best. It is a sour-style drink, meaning it contains spirit, sweet, and citrus. Honey makes a wonderful ingredient in cocktails. To incorporate honey into the cocktail more easily, mix two parts honey to one part boiled hot water and let it cool. This will thin it out a bit, creating a honey syrup. Most drinks with citrus are shaken, not stirred, and that is the case here.

INGREDIENTS & METHOD

Add the gin, lemon juice, and honey syrup to the shaker with ice. **Shake** vigorously until very cold, about 15 seconds. **Strain** into the chilled glass. **Hold** the twist lengthwise just over the glass in the thumb and index finger of each hand and gently fold to express the oils from the peel. **Rub** the twist on the rim of the glass and discard the twist.

TIP Honey comes in many varieties. We encourage you to explore different types of honey and be sure to taste your drink before serving to others because sweetness levels vary.

Piña Colada,
page 60

6

Rum

Rum is made in almost every corner of the world, in many different styles. Rum was first produced in the American colonial era; some historical accounts claim the tax on rum was a bigger problem for the colonists than the tax on tea. Rum is usually produced from molasses, the by-product of making granulated sugar. The exceptions are rhum agricole from Martinique and cachaça from Brazil, both made from sugar cane juice. A renewed interest in tiki culture is boosting rum sales. Types of rum include silver rum, which is either unaged or aged then filtered, but there are many delicious aged (dark) rums available, too. Many of these are wonderful to sip neat with a little ice, or as a substitute for traditional whiskey in drinks such as an Old Fashioned. Limes and rum belong together, as you'll see in several of our recipes here, but this spirit can also stand up to bold flavors including ginger, passion fruit, nuts, and more.

daiquiri

GLASSWARE & TOOLS

- Coupe or martini glass (chilled)
- Citrus juicer
- Jigger
- Shaker
- Hawthorne strainer

The Daiquiri is generally credited to Jennings Cox, an American engineer in Cuba during the Spanish-American War. Cox may have created the cocktail to prevent yellow fever in his workers or when he ran out of gin during a party. While the frozen Daiquiri can be a delightful drink, the classic Daiquiri is served up, meaning the ingredients are chilled and served in a cocktail glass. Because this drink is made with just three ingredients, the trick here is to use high-quality products and the proper techniques to get the balance just right. This drink is a favorite of bartenders, as it allows them to show off their skills, and it's delicious.

INGREDIENTS & METHOD

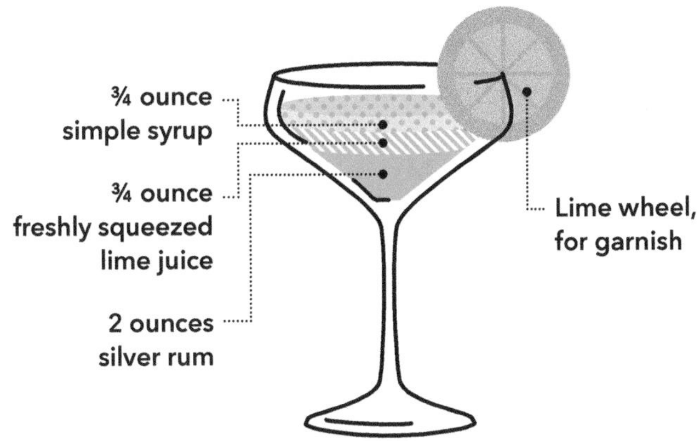

Pour the simple syrup, lime juice and rum into the shaker. **Add** ice. **Shake** until very cold, about 15 seconds. **Strain** into the chilled glass. **Garnish** with a lime wheel.

By mastering this basic sour drink, you'll have a solid jumping-off point for a myriad of other cocktails: the Margarita, the Mai Tai, and the Whiskey Sour. Add club soda to a sour cocktail and a whole new world of drinks emerges, such as the Mojito and the Tom Collins.

mojito

GLASSWARE & TOOLS

- Highball glass (12-ounce, ideally)
- Citrus juicer
- Jigger
- Muddler
- Bar spoon
- Shaker
- Fine strainer
- Hawthorne strainer

If you make the classic Daiquiri, add some mint and club soda, and serve it over ice, you have the Mojito. The origins of this drink are generally traced back to Havana, Cuba, but it's hard to know who invented it. One story says it was a health tonic made for the crew of Sir Francis Drake in the 1500s by locals, and another credits African slaves who worked in the Cuban fields. Hemingway's favorite bar, La Bodeguita del Medio, claims the version they made for him is responsible for its popularity. The drink was also featured in a beach scene in the Bond film *Die Another Day*.

INGREDIENTS & METHOD

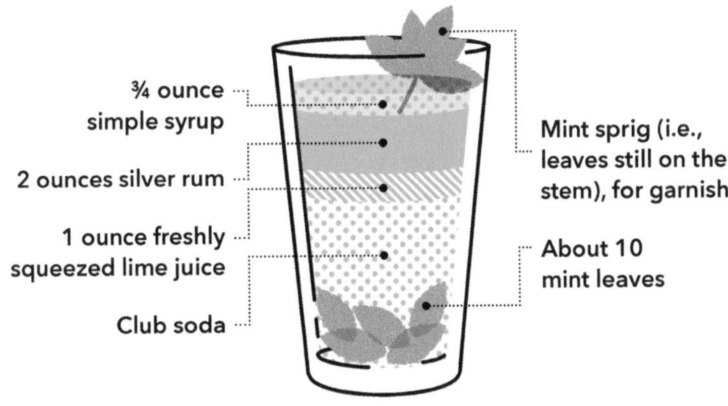

Put the mint leaves in the smaller mixing tin. Using a muddler, gently press on the leaves to release the oils. **Add** the simple syrup. **Mix** gently with the muddler. **Add** the rum and lime juice. **Fill** the larger mixing tin with ice. **Pour** the contents from the smaller mixing tin into the larger tin. **Shake** vigorously until very cold, about 15 seconds. **Allow** all the ingredients to remain in the large tin. **Fill** a Highball glass with ice. **Double strain:** Place the Hawthorne strainer on the large tin, hold the fine strainer over the Highball glass, and then pour through both strainers. **Top** with the club soda. **Stir gently** to combine, two or three rotations. **Garnish** with a mint sprig.

TIP	Don't be aggressive when muddling the mint leaves, as it makes the herb bitter. Gently press on the leaves with a muddler to release the fragrant oils. The stems of the mint leaves can sometimes have a "woody" character; it's best to avoid them if you can.

mai tai

GLASSWARE & TOOLS

Old fashioned glass

Citrus juicer/ extractor

Jigger for measuring

Shaker

Hawthorne strainer

The name "mai tai" most likely comes from the Tahitian saying "mai tai roa," which more or less means "out of this world." The origin story of the Mai Tai is similarly out of this world as two people claim they invented the tropical cocktail. Victor Bergeron claims to have invented the Mai Tai in 1944 at his California restaurant Trader Vic's. But, Donn Beach of Don the Beachcomber claims that recipe was a copy of his own similar-tasting creation, the Q.B. Cooler. Our Mai Tai recipe tastes like the tropics, balancing the rum against the citrus from the lime, orange flavors from the curaçao, and an unexpected twist from the orgeat, an almond syrup. One sip of this tasty Mai Tai and you'll be transported to the tropics!

INGREDIENTS & METHOD

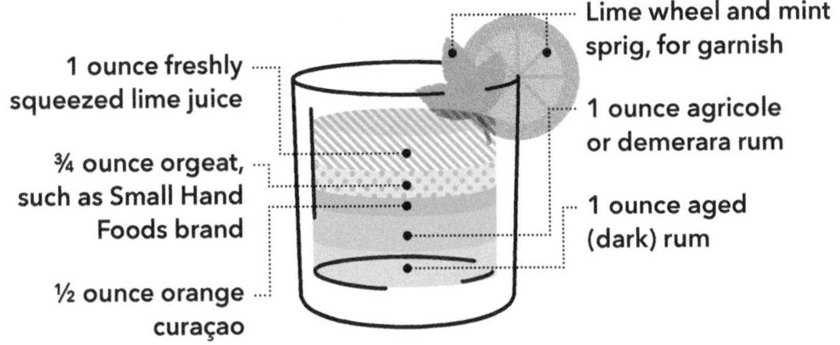

Pour the lime juice, orgeat, curaçao or almond extract, and rum into the shaker. **Add** ice. **Shake** until very cold, about 15 seconds. **Fill** the glass with fresh ice and strain into it. **Garnish** with the lime wheel and mint sprig.

TIP It's ideal to use a Jamaican rum, such as Plantation Rum Jamaica or Appleton's Estate. For the orange curaçao, Pierre Ferrand or Cointreau is best. And if you don't have orgeat, you can use ¾ ounce of simple syrup and a drop of almond extract.

caipirinha

GLASSWARE & TOOLS

- Old fashioned glass
- Jigger
- Muddler

The Caipirinha (kai/pee/reen/ya) is the national drink of Brazil. The base spirit cachaça (ka/cha/sa) is made from sugar and considered to be in the rum family, but it is much more vegetal and earthy than other styles of rum. Though it is served in an old fashioned glass, this drink is very informal. While we encourage you to measure all the ingredients carefully for most cocktails, this one is free-styled. Once you master it, you can have a great time teaching friends how to make it at a party. Put out a bowl of cut limes, some sugar, and a bottle of cachaça, and show everyone the fun new drink you learned and how they can easily make it, too.

INGREDIENTS & METHOD

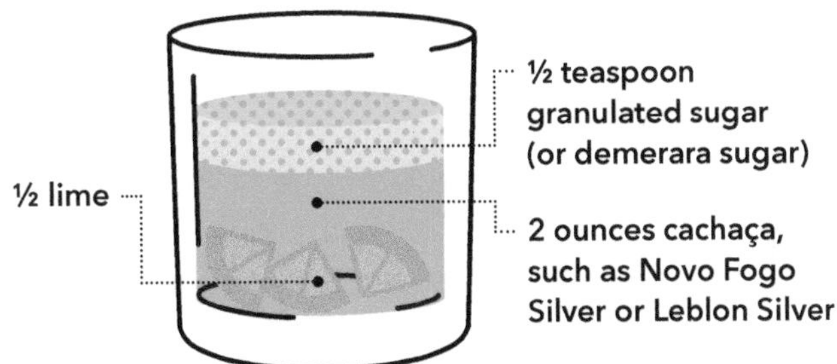

Place half a lime cut-side down on a cutting board and cut about ⅛ inch off the "north and south poles," or the ends. **Cut** the half lime into three wedges (or four wedges for a large lime). **Cut** each wedge in half widthwise to make almost a cube, the ideal shape. **Put** six lime "cubes" in the old fashioned glass. **Add** the sugar. **Use** the muddler to extract the juice and incorporate the sugar. **Add** the cachaça. **Stir** with the muddler to incorporate. **Add** ice to fill the glass.

TIP If the funkiness (or soil-like flavor) of the cachaça puts you off, or if you have a difficult time finding it, substitute a traditional silver rum of your choice, such as the ubiquitous Bacardi Silver.

piña colada

GLASSWARE & TOOLS

Hurricane glass (or whatever large glass you have on hand)

Blender

Declared the official drink of Puerto Rico in 1978, the Piña Colada's creation is contested by two San Juan spots: Barrachina Restaurant and Caribe Hilton. But it was Caribe Hilton that received the birthplace proclamation on its 50th anniversary by the Puerto Rican governor. Piña Coladas are a decadent treat and Coco Lopez Cream of Coconut is hard to beat for this drink. To keep it simple, we use equal parts coconut cream, pineapple juice, and rum. Note that Piña Coladas are best when shared and this recipe makes generous portions for two people.

INGREDIENTS & METHOD

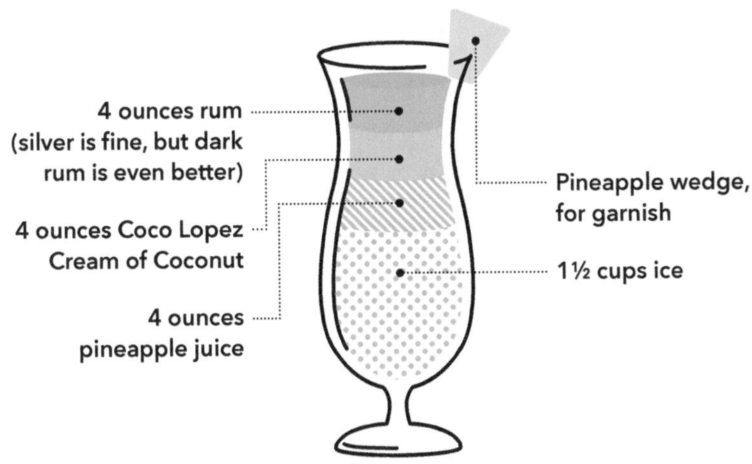

Blend the rum, cream of coconut, and pineapple juice with ice until smooth and creamy. Throw a pineapple wedge or two in the blender, too, if you like. **Pour** into whatever glassware is desired. **Garnish** with the pineapple wedge. You'll need a straw (preferably paper) for this one.

TIP Plantation Rum's Plantation Stiggins' Fancy Pineapple is made with real pineapples, not artificial flavoring. It is outrageously good in a Piña Colada, as we learned firsthand at a rooftop bar in Manhattan a couple of summers back.

Tequila Sunrise,
page 70

7

Tequila

Tequila is earthy and a bit malty, and it often has vanilla and/or caramel notes. It's quite a funky spirit. For a product to be labeled "tequila," it must be produced in specific regions in Mexico. There is one very important thing to know when purchasing tequila: To get a quality product, the words "100% agave" must be on the label. There are variations on this, but if it doesn't indicate some combination of "100% agave" on the label, it means it is blended with lesser-quality alcohols and is most likely an inferior product. Silver tequila plays well with bright citrus flavors such as lime and grapefruit. While the aged reposado and añejo can make interesting variations on Margarita-style drinks, they can also stand in for whisk(e)y in boozy cocktails.

margarita

GLASSWARE & TOOLS

Served on the rocks: an old fashioned glass or rocks glass

Served up: a margarita glass, coupe, or martini glass (chilled)

Citrus juicer/ extractor

Jigger

Shaker

Strainer

The Margarita continues to be America's favorite cocktail (or so says the Nielsen ratings company), however its history remains obscure, with credit going from Dallas socialite Margarita Sames to a claim by Pancho Morales, a Mexican bartender turned truck driver. While many bars and restaurants opt to use artificial sour mix, once you try our version of this recipe, you'll be converted. Then the questions to ask are: Up or on the rocks? Salt or no salt? We prefer our Margaritas on the rocks but encourage you to explore.

INGREDIENTS & METHOD

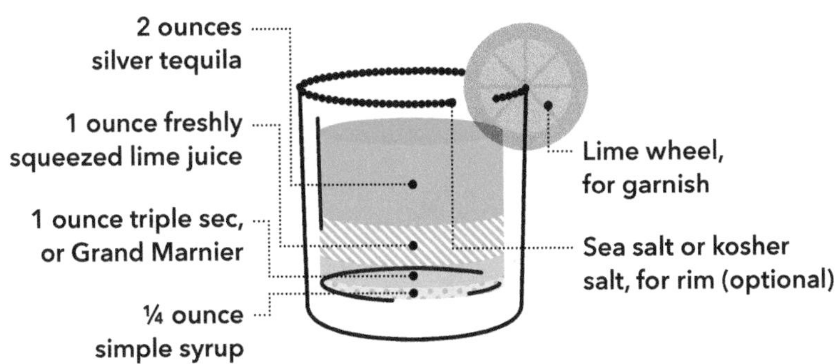

If a salted rim is desired, the first step is to moisten the outside of the rim of your glass with a lime wedge. **Dip** the glass into a dish filled with salt. The salt rim layer should be very thin and only on the outside of the glass. If you decide on a salt rim, coat only half the glass with salt to give the drinker a choice, unless a salt rim was requested. **Set** the glass aside. **Fill** the shaker halfway with ice and add the tequila, lime juice, triple sec, and simple syrup. **Shake** for 15 seconds, then strain into a chilled glass if serving up or into a double old fashioned glass filled with fresh ice. **Garnish** with the lime wheel.

If you're feeling fancy, use añejo tequila and high-quality Grand Marnier over triple sec (½ ounce) with the simple syrup to produce a heavier mouthfeel. You've now made a Cadillac Margarita.

paloma

GLASSWARE & TOOLS

Highball glass

Citrus juicer/ extractor

Jigger

Shaker

Strainer

It is said that the Paloma, which means "dove" in Spanish, is more popular in Mexico than the Margarita. While its exact origin remains unknown, stories of its creation vary from Don Javier, owner of the La Capilla bar in Tequila, Mexico, to US bartender Evan Harrison, to a pamphlet titled "Popular Cocktails of the Rio Grande," to the American grapefruit soda Squirt. It's a simple drink to make, although we give you a fancier and fresher variation here.

INGREDIENTS & METHOD

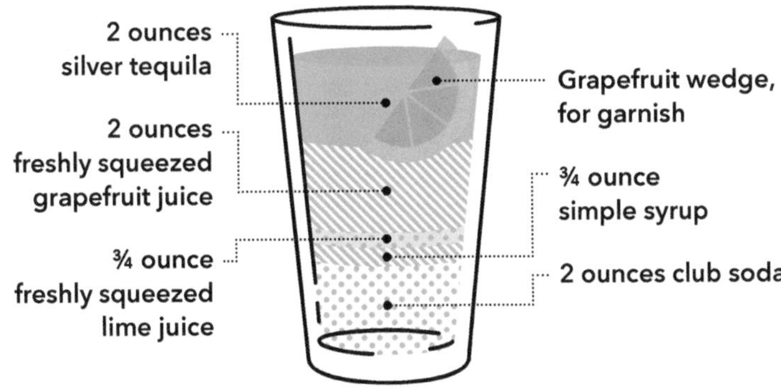

Pour the tequila, grapefruit juice, lime juice, and simple syrup into a shaker with ice and shake until very cold, about 15 seconds. **Add** the club soda to the shaker. **Strain** into the Highball glass filled with fresh ice. **Submerge** the grapefruit wedge in the glass and serve.

el diablo

GLASSWARE & TOOLS

- Highball glass
- Citrus juicer/extractor
- Jigger
- Shaker
- Strainer

El Diablo means "the devil" in Spanish, but don't be scared of this cocktail. It's a delicious drink with flavors that will impress your friends. In 1946, El Diablo first appeared in print as the "Mexican Diablo," but it is probably older than that. Similar to the Mai Tai, this is another cocktail created by Trader Vic. This drink calls for a reposado tequila (tequila that has been aged in oak), and it certainly benefits from the extra flavor that spirit delivers; but if you only have a silver tequila on hand, it's still worth giving this drink a try.

INGREDIENTS & METHOD

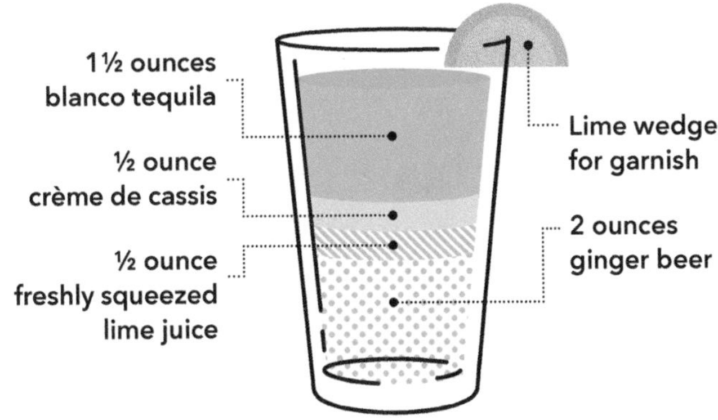

Pour the tequila, crème de cassis, and lime juice into a shaker with ice and shake. **Strain** into the glass containing fresh ice. **Add** ginger beer to fill the glass. **Stir** gently, about three rotations. **Garnish** with the lime wedge.

tequila sunrise

GLASSWARE & TOOLS

- Highball glass
- Citrus juicer/ extractor
- Jigger
- Bar spoon

The Tequila Sunrise is a drink from the 1970s, and like most drinks created in that era, it's incredibly sweet and pretty to look at. For our modern take on the Tequila Sunrise, we like to add freshly squeezed orange juice, a quality tequila, and homemade grenadine. Unlike the versions available in the store, real grenadine is made from pomegranates; it is not at all difficult to make, and we've provided a recipe.

INGREDIENTS & METHOD

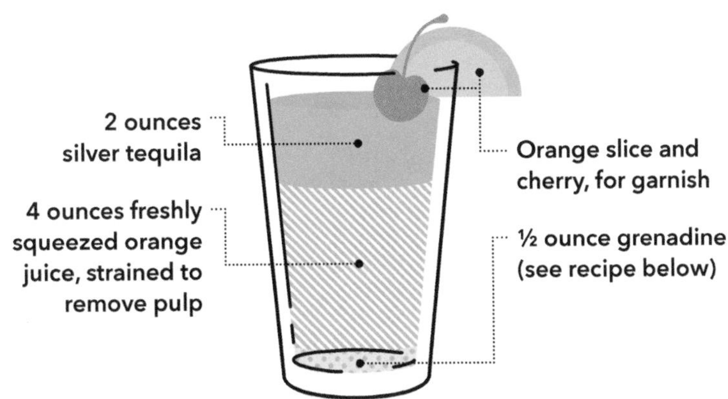

Add the tequila and orange juice to an ice-filled Highball glass. **Stir** gently, about three rotations. **Add** the grenadine; it will sink to the bottom, as it should. **Garnish** with the orange slice and cherry.

Fresh Grenadine Recipe

Combine equal parts POM Wonderful Pomegranate Juice and sugar. Stir as the sugar settles and it'll be ready to use in 15 minutes.

matador

GLASSWARE & TOOLS

Martini glass or champagne flute (chilled)

Citrus juicer/ extractor

Jigger

Shaker

Strainer

The Matador cocktail is a close cousin to the Margarita, but the addition of aromatic bitters adds a spicy and herbal note. The pineapple juice adds fruitiness and contains enzymes that, with vigorous shaking, create a nice foamy head for the cocktail. Usually served up in a martini glass or champagne flute, this drink mirrors the theatrical golden hue of the embroidery on a real matador's suit.

INGREDIENTS & METHOD

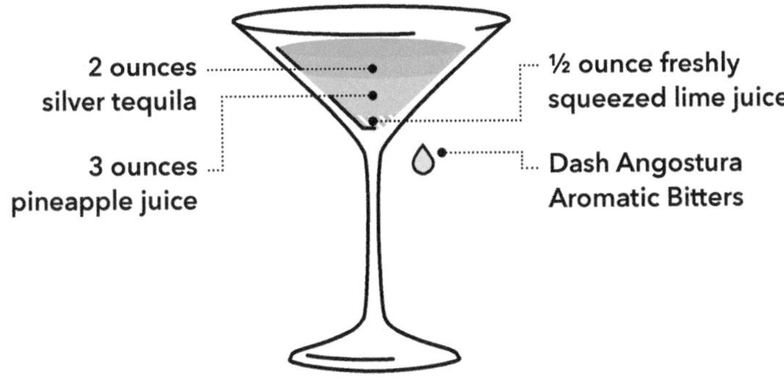

Pour the tequila, pineapple juice, bitters, and lime juice into the shaker. **Shake** with ice until very cold, about 15 seconds. **Strain** into a chilled martini glass or champagne flute.

Bloody Mary,
page 82

8

Vodka

Vodka is a versatile spirit simply because it doesn't have a dominant flavor. While there are numerous flavored vodkas available (of varied quality), an unflavored vodka can add a kick when paired with most any fruit juice or soda. Some cocktail enthusiasts enjoy a vodka Martini, but our preferred Martini recipe skews more traditional and uses gin. Depending on what you are craving, you can use the Martini recipe in this book and substitute vodka for gin. Go with what you like, and above all, enjoy!

cosmopolitan

GLASSWARE & TOOLS

Martini glass (chilled)

Citrus juicer/ extractor

Jigger

Shaker

Strainer

The standard recipe for the Cosmopolitan, or Cosmo, is generally credited to New York City–based bartender Toby Cecchini of the Odeon, circa 1988. Dale DeGroff ("The King of Cocktails") had a pivotal role in popularizing this drink when he put his version on the menu at the Rainbow Room in New York. Media featured photos of Madonna drinking one at the Rainbow Room during a 1995 Grammy party, and after that, everyone wanted one. Later, the cocktail's debut on the HBO show *Sex and the City* in 1998 turned it into a modern classic. This recipe is the one Dale DeGroff standardized.

INGREDIENTS & METHOD

Fill the shaker halfway with ice and add the cranberry juice, lime juice, vodka, and Cointreau. **Shake** vigorously for 15 seconds, then strain into a chilled martini glass. **Garnish** with the lime wheel.

Brian Weber's Cosmo
Use 2 ounces of unflavored vodka in place of citrus vodka, ½ ounce of Grand Marnier instead of Cointreau, and increase the amount of lime juice to ¾ ounce. Adding ¼ ounce of simple syrup rounds it out and adds a little weight to the liquid.

moscow mule

GLASSWARE & TOOLS

- Copper mug or Highball glass
- Jigger
- Bar spoon

The Moscow Mule is not only an easy cocktail to enjoy at a bar, but it's also incredibly easy to make at home. The Moscow Mule is traditionally served in a copper mug, a practice that can be traced back to a man named John G. Martin, whose beverage distribution company purchased the rights to Smirnoff Vodka for $14,000 in 1939. At the time, vodka was very rare in the United States, as Americans were mostly whiskey drinkers, so Martin traveled around the country taking Polaroid photos of bartenders posing with copper mugs and a bottle of Smirnoff to try to entice drinkers. The marketing campaign was a success and the preference to serve Moscow Mules in copper mugs continues to this day.

INGREDIENTS & METHOD

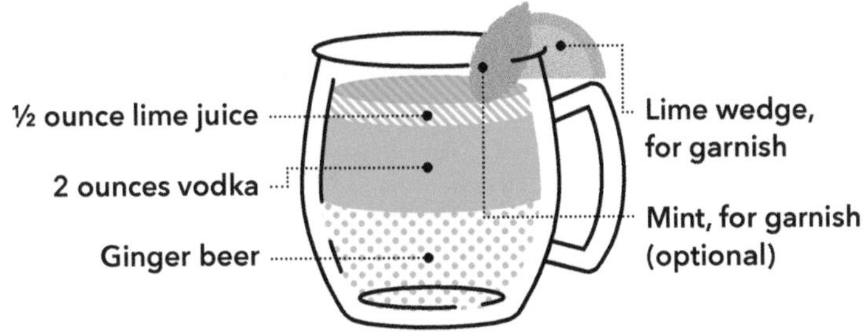

Fill the mug or glass with ice. **Add** the lime juice and vodka. **Fill** the glass with ginger beer. **Stir** gently with the bar spoon to combine, about three rotations. **Garnish** with the lime wedge and mint (if using).

white russian

GLASSWARE & TOOLS

Old fashioned glass

Jigger

Two-piece shaker set or two pint glasses

Strainer

This drink is not Russian in origin; rather, it seems to have originated in the United States in the years after World War II. Americans associated vodka with Russia, so the name seems to have stemmed from that. If you've ever seen *The Big Lebowski* starring Jeff Bridges, you know that when "the Dude abides," he enjoys a White Russian, and it helped the drink gain popularity. You may see pretty White Russians in bars or photos online where the drink has a layered effect. While we admit it does look nice, we choose to incorporate all the ingredients together so that it actually *tastes* good.

INGREDIENTS & METHOD

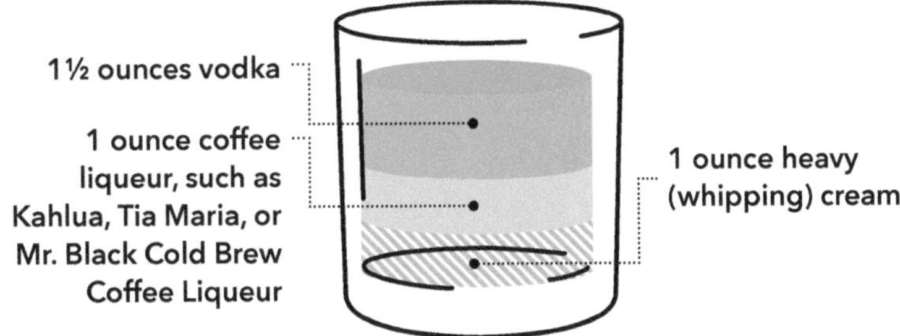

Pour the vodka, coffee liqueur, and heavy cream into a cocktail shaker or pint glass. **Add** ice. **Roll** the drink from one cocktail shaker or pint glass to the other to combine, then back into the first to combine. **Strain** into an ice-filled old fashioned glass.

TIP For a lighter version of this cocktail, add a splash of club soda (known as a Smith & Kearns), and/or switch the heavy cream for light cream or milk.

bloody mary

GLASSWARE & TOOLS

Highball glass

Jigger

Two-piece shaker set or two pint glasses

Strainer

It is widely accepted that the Bloody Mary was invented around 1920 at the New York Bar in Paris, France. This is the perfect cocktail for getting creative: You can always create variations by looking into your spice cabinet for new flavor combinations or checking your refrigerator for elaborate garnishes. Our recipe is a great starting point, but we recommend making the mix (without the booze) and tasting it first. Is it missing anything that might make it more interesting? We love adding unexpected ingredients that can really transform this cocktail, like freshly squeezed lemon juice or horseradish. If you are having a brunch gathering, make a large batch of "Virgin Mary" ahead of time, and add the booze to order.

INGREDIENTS & METHOD

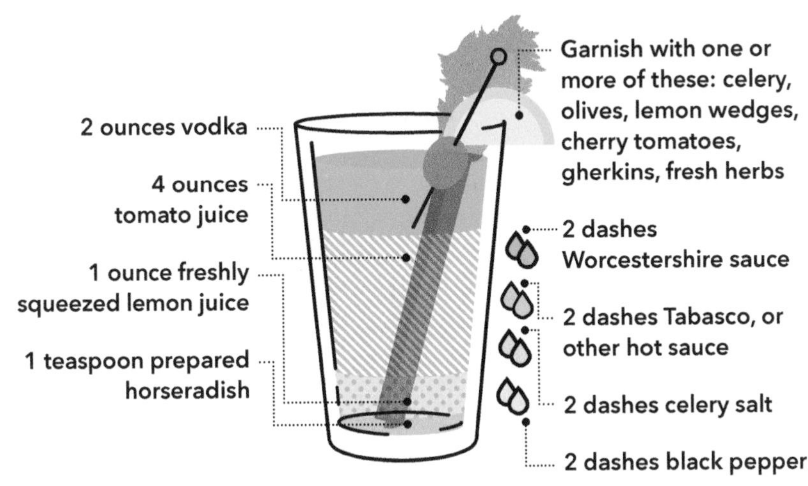

Put the vodka, tomato juice, lemon juice, horseradish, Worcestershire sauce, Tabasco, celery salt, and black pepper in a cocktail shaker or pint glass. **Add** ice. **Roll** the drink from one cocktail shaker or pint glass to the other to combine, then back into the first to combine. **Strain** into an ice-filled Highball glass. **Garnish** as desired.

TIP Try these additional flavorings in your Bloody Mary: Old Bay seasoning, olive brine, pickle juice, paprika, red Hawaiian sea salt dissolved in a little hot water, garlic powder, onion powder. For an explosion of flavors, substitute vodka with silver tequila for a Bloody Maria.

espresso martini

GLASSWARE & TOOLS

- Martini glass (chilled)
- Jigger
- Shaker
- Strainer

We try to avoid the "anything served in a martini glass can be called a Martini" mania, however, the Espresso Martini cocktail is a decadent treat. It was invented in the 1980s by the late English bartender Dick Bradsell. According to Bradsell, he created this cocktail for a model who wanted "something that would wake her up, then f@#$ her up." Bradsell's recipe calls for a little simple syrup, but you can simplify things a bit by leaving out the syrup and slightly increasing the amount of coffee liqueur. A 1.5:1:1 ratio works well. Of course, the strength of the espresso can vary, so you may want to adjust according to your tastes.

INGREDIENTS & METHOD

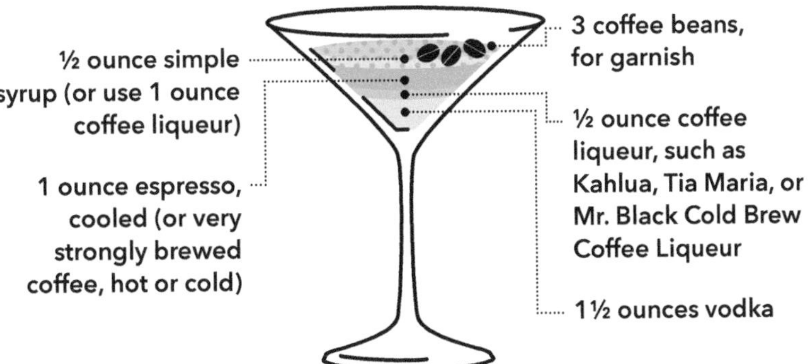

Pour the simple syrup, espresso, coffee liqueur, and vodka into the shaker. **Add** ice and shake until very cold, about 15 seconds. **Strain** into a chilled martini glass. **Float** the coffee beans on top.

TIP For a delicious and fun mash-up of an Espresso Martini and an Irish Coffee, substitute Irish whiskey for vodka.

Old Fashioned,
page 88

9

Whisk(e)y

Whiskey/whisky is made all over the world in a variety of styles. In all its forms, it's wonderful to drink neat, with a little ice, or as the base spirit in a cocktail. Bourbon, made only in the United States, is made primarily from corn and picks up hints of caramel, vanilla, and other flavors from being aged in an oak barrel. Scotch whisky is known for being smoky, but there are a variety of flavor profiles. Irish whiskey, which is making a huge comeback, is slightly sweeter and rounder in its flavor. Rye whiskey is a little spicy (think of rye bread) and delicious. Whisk(e)y is a diverse category which leads to a broad range of cocktails that can be created from this wonderful spirit. The possibilities are endless (and tasty)!

old fashioned

GLASSWARE & TOOLS

Old fashioned glass or rocks glass

Mixing glass

Jigger

Bar spoon

Julep strainer

Vegetable peeler

In 1806, *The Balance and Columbian Repository*, a New York newspaper, defined a cocktail as "spirits of any kind, sugar, water, and bitters." A perfect example of this is the Old Fashioned. In 1888, the first known recipe for the Old Fashioned appeared in *The Bartender's Manual* by Theodore Proulx, and it was already an "old" cocktail by then. The Old Fashioned has come and gone many times within our drinking history but was resurrected by the television show *Mad Men* and mastered by bartenders who refused to create anything other than the pre-Prohibition version. We love the Old Fashioned because it is simple to make and really allows the character of the whiskey to shine through.

INGREDIENTS & METHOD

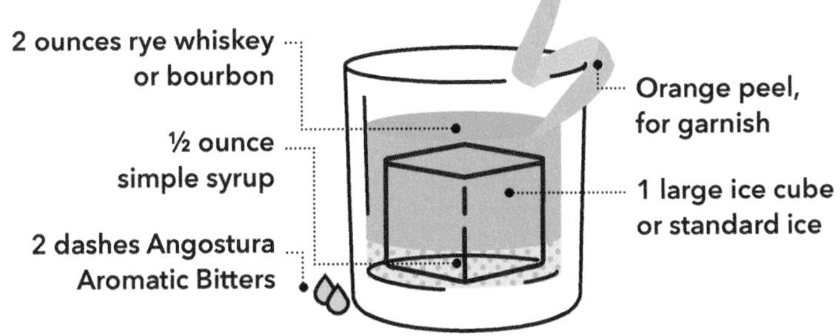

Pour the whiskey, simple syrup, and bitters into the mixing glass. **Add** ice and stir until very cold, about 15 seconds. **Strain** into the glass over new ice. **Using** the peeler, make an orange twist about 2 inches long. **Express** the oils from the peel, rub the twist on the rim, and put into the drink.

For a decadent variation, try maple simple syrup. Combine 1 cup each of maple syrup and water in a saucepan. Add a few whole cloves, 1 teaspoon each of allspice and cardamom, or similar spices. Add a pinch of sea salt. Boil until it is reduced by about half. Let cool.

TIP Use black walnut bitters from Fee Brothers in place of the Angostura Aromatic Bitters.

manhattan

GLASSWARE & TOOLS

Coupe or martini glass (chilled)

Jigger

Mixing glass

Bar spoon

Strainer

Bartenders really appreciate when a guest orders this classic cocktail. It has a long history that appears to date back to the 1880s at the Manhattan Club. The recipe is a simple 2:1 formula of whiskey to sweet vermouth, plus bitters. Which whiskey should you use? Rye is classic. It's a fine drink with bourbon as well, though it is possible for it to be too sweet, so consider using slightly less vermouth if you prefer a Manhattan made with bourbon. Manhattans are usually topped off with a cherry (we recommend the best quality maraschino cherries you can find, such as Luxardo), although an orange twist is not out of place. Or go for the unexpected: A lemon twist really brightens up this drink.

INGREDIENTS & METHOD

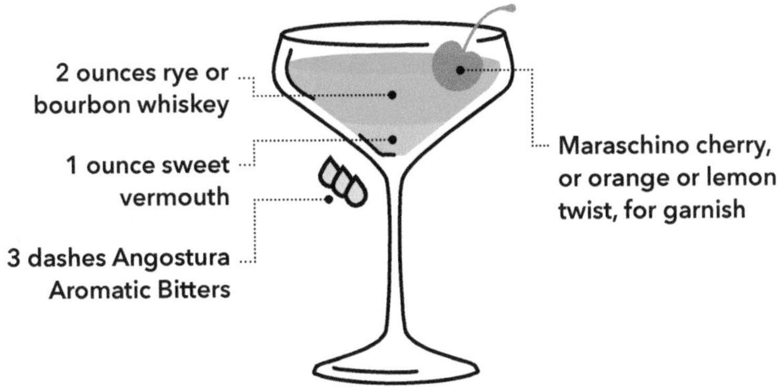

Pour the whiskey, vermouth, and bitters into the mixing glass. **Add** ice until the glass is about two-thirds full. **Stir** until very cold, about 15 seconds. **Strain** into the chilled glass. If using a twist, express the oils from the peel, rub on the rim, and put in the cocktail. If using a cherry, simply drop it into the glass.

This drink is always *stirred. In our opinion, there is nothing less appealing than a Manhattan that has been shaken.*

whiskey sour

GLASSWARE & TOOLS

- Old fashioned glass
- Jigger
- Shaker
- Strainer

The Whiskey Sour first appeared in print in 1862 in Jerry Thomas's book *The Bar-tender's Guide* (alternately titled *The Bon-Vivant's Companion*). Thomas was somewhat of a celebrity bartender in his time and he was the first to write down many classic cocktail recipes. As the name of this cocktail implies, the Whiskey Sour belongs to the sour family, meaning it is made from just three ingredients: spirit, citrus, and sugar. Pretty much any American whiskey will work here. The citrus in the formula is freshly squeezed lemon juice and the sugar is simple syrup. There is an option to add an egg white, which adds a pleasant, frothy head to the cocktail.

INGREDIENTS & METHOD

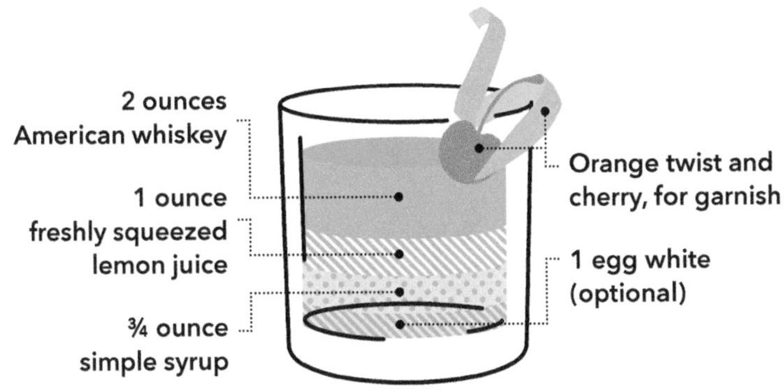

Pour the whiskey, lemon juice, simple syrup, and egg white (if using) into the shaker. **Add** ice and double shake. If you are not including the egg white, shake all the ingredients until very cold, about 15 seconds. **Strain** into the glass containing fresh ice. **Garnish** with the orange twist and cherry.

A tasty variation: Use ½ ounce of lemon juice and ½ ounce of lime juice instead of only lemon juice.

mint julep

GLASSWARE & TOOLS

Metal julep cup or old fashioned glass

Jigger

Muddler

This cocktail most likely originated as a medicinal drink in England, but it is now thought of as a classic cocktail of the American South. Each year at the Kentucky Derby, about 120,000 Mint Juleps are sold. Using fresh mint is key, and when you muddle it, do so gently—just enough to release the oils from the skins. Smashing the mint to pieces makes it bitter and unattractive. Some bartenders like to use superfine sugar or even powdered sugar. We like to use simple syrup for several reasons; for one thing, there is no risk of leaving undissolved sugar behind.

INGREDIENTS & METHOD

Place the mint leaves in the bottom of the cup. **Press** lightly on them with the muddler to release the oils from the leaves. **Add** the simple syrup and gently muddle again to incorporate. **Add** the whiskey and, using the muddler or a spoon, stir to combine. **Pack** with as much crushed ice as possible. **Garnish** with the mint sprig. If using a straw, cut it short so that the mint is close to your nose as you drink, as the aromas are part of the experience.

TIP

If you're planning a Kentucky Derby party, you can make a mint syrup in advance to save time. In a saucepan, combine 1 cup each of sugar and water. Bring to a boil, stirring occasionally. Remove from the heat and add a generous handful of mint leaves. Let cool for about 45 minutes. Using a mesh strainer, strain and refrigerate in a glass or plastic container. Mint syrup will keep for about a week.

irish coffee

GLASSWARE & TOOLS

Georgian Irish coffee glass or footed Irish coffee mug (heated)

Jigger

Bar spoon

Milk frother or whisk for thickening cream

Irish Coffee is an Irish-American cocktail that became wildly popular in the 1950s at the Buena Vista Cafe, where the drink is still served—roughly 2,000 per day. Buena Vista Cafe uses one of our favorite Irish whiskeys, Tullamore Dew, but almost any brand will do. Try this version for a break from your traditional cup of morning coffee if you're feeling adventurous, or as a warm, cozy cocktail in the colder months.

INGREDIENTS & METHOD

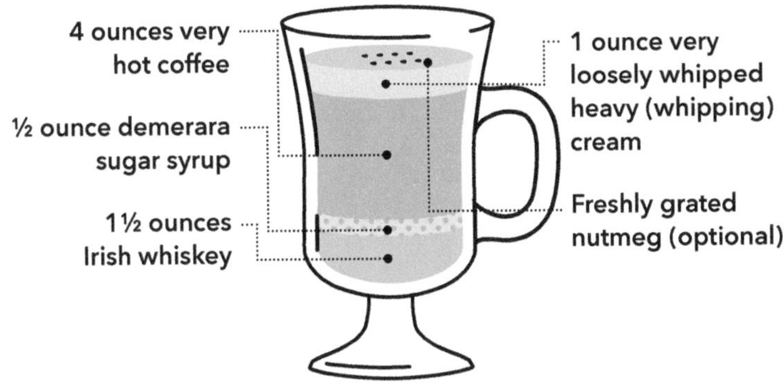

Brew the coffee before you make the drink. **Heat** the cup or mug with boiling hot water for at least 30 seconds. **Pour** out the hot water. **Pour** in the sugar syrup and whiskey. **Top** with the hot coffee, leaving about ¾ inch for cream. **Gently** pour the loosely whipped cream over the back of the bar spoon so that it floats on top of the drink. **Grate** a little fresh nutmeg (if using) and sprinkle it over the drink. **Serve** immediately.

TIP The whipped heavy cream should be frothy but not what we think of as whipped cream–just loose enough to pour.

Sidecar,
page 100

10

Brandy

Brandy can be produced from any fruit, but it is most commonly made from grapes. Cognac, for instance, is a grape brandy produced in the Cognac region of France. Brandy is produced all over the world. For example, the company Copper & Kings is producing wonderful grape brandies in bourbon country in Louisville, Kentucky. Or take applejack, a brandy made from apples. Brandy is largely thought of as a spirit to drink neat after dinner, but it is actually a wonderful and versatile ingredient in cocktails. It can match well with bright citrus flavors and works in a creamy sweet drink like the Brandy Alexander.

sidecar

GLASSWARE & TOOLS

Coupe or martini glass (chilled)

Citrus juicer/ extractor

Jigger

Shaker

Hawthorne strainer

Vegetable peeler

This drink emerged after the end of World War I, with stories citing its origin in either the Ritz Hotel in Paris or the Buck's Club in London. The Sidecar appears in Harry MacElhone's *Harry's ABC of Mixing Cocktails* and Robert Vermeire's *Cocktails and How to Mix Them*, both published in the early 1920s. Named for the sidecar that attaches to a motorcycle for an extra passenger, it is a fairly boozy drink, so we hope the motorcycle driver stays away from the Sidecar cocktail! It can be served in a sugar-rimmed glass, but it doesn't really need that extra sweetness.

INGREDIENTS & METHOD

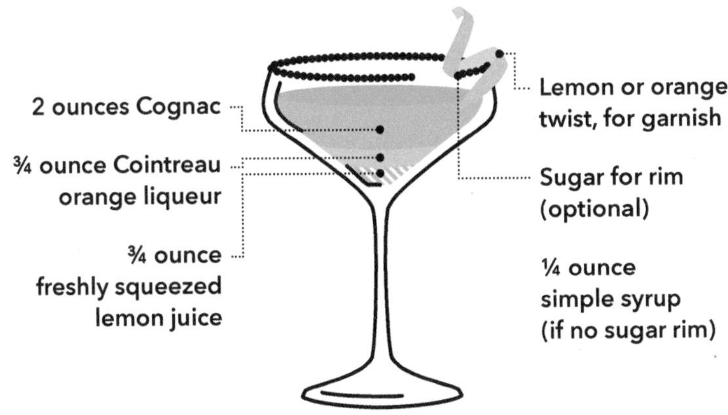

If using a sugar rim, rim the chilled glass before creating the cocktail. **Fill** the shaker halfway with ice and add the Cognac, Cointreau, and lemon juice (include the simple syrup now if not using a sugar rim). **Shake** until very cold, about 15 seconds. **Strain** into the chilled glass. **Garnish** with the lemon or orange twist.

Use 1 ounce of Cognac and 1 ounce of aged (dark) rum instead of 2 ounces of Cognac and you have a flirty "Between the Sheets" cocktail.

corpse reviver

GLASSWARE & TOOLS

- Coupe or martini glass (chilled)
- Mixing cup
- Jigger
- Bar spoon
- Strainer

There are many variations of this cocktail, designated by number. We present here the Corpse Reviver No. 1, which features two different types of brandies: Cognac and apple brandy (which can be American applejack or French Calvados). The Corpse Reviver No. 2 is quite different, using gin as the base and no brandy at all. Whatever the recipe, the Corpse Reviver cocktail is meant to be a morning-after drink, as you may have guessed from the name. Harry Craddock's *The Savoy Cocktail Book,* published in 1930, states, "Four of these taken in swift succession will un-revive the corpse again," so drink responsibly.

INGREDIENTS & METHOD

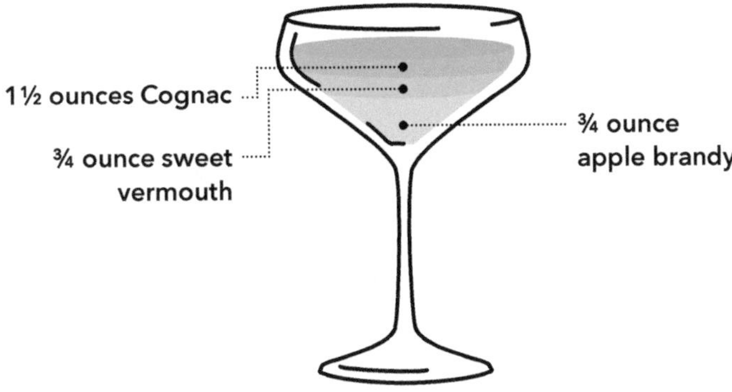

Pour the sweet vermouth, brandy, and Cognac into the mixing glass. **Stir** all the ingredients with ice until very cold, about 15 seconds. **Strain** into the chilled glass.

BRANDY

jack rose

GLASSWARE & TOOLS

Coupe or martini glass (chilled)

Shaker

Jigger

Strainer

Applejack is brandy made from apples in the United States. It seems that the first half of this cocktail's name, Jack, comes from applejack. The second half, rose, comes from the color imparted by the grenadine. However, there are also stories out there that say the drink was named for a person called Jack Rose. This cocktail was popular during the Prohibition era, and in fact it makes an appearance in Ernest Hemingway's classic novel *The Sun Also Rises* (1926). The Jack Rose was also a favorite of author John Steinbeck. Lemon or lime juice can be used here, but we find the lemon version more delicate.

INGREDIENTS & METHOD

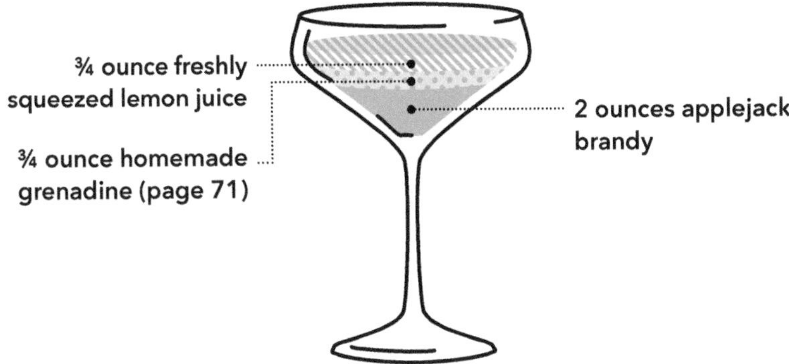

Pour the lemon juice, grenadine, and brandy into the shaker. **Shake** all the ingredients vigorously with ice until very cold, about 15 seconds. **Strain** into the chilled glass.

Apple brandy was first produced in colonial New Jersey in 1698 by William Laird. Laird's applejack was granted federal liquor license no. 1. Another great brand of applejack is Black Dirt, produced in the lower Hudson Valley of New York.

pisco sour

GLASSWARE & TOOLS

Coupe, martini glass, or champagne flute (chilled)

Shaker

Jigger

Strainer

Pisco is a brandy distilled from fermented grape juice in both Peru and Chile. So which country did this cocktail originate from? The answer is both. At one time both territories were under common rule by the Spanish. A 1921 magazine article credited the invention of the cocktail to American bartender Victor Vaughen Morris, who was working in Peru at the time. In the modern era, the Pisco Sour is considered to be the national drink of both Peru and Chile. In Chile the drink is made with pisco, lime juice, and simple syrup. The Peruvian version adds egg white and Angostura Aromatic Bitters. We encourage you to try both!

INGREDIENTS & METHOD

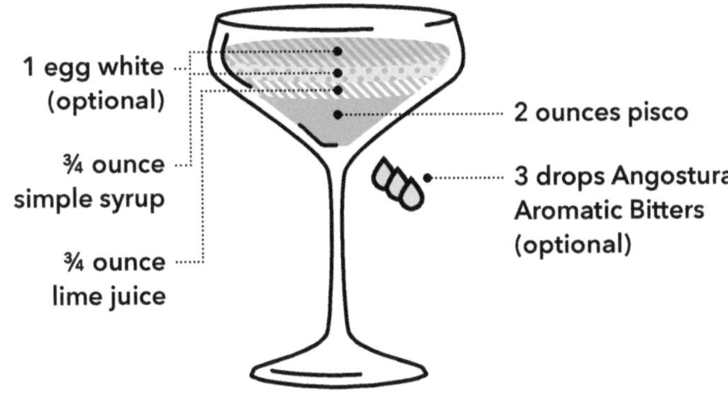

Pour the egg white (if using), simple syrup, lime juice, and pisco into the shaker. **Shake** all the ingredients with ice vigorously until very cold, about 15 seconds (shake a few seconds longer if using egg whites, to create frothiness). **Strain** into the chilled glass. **Garnish** with three drops of bitters (if using).

brandy alexander

GLASSWARE & TOOLS

Coupe or martini glass (chilled)

Shaker

Jigger

Strainer

It is difficult to pin down the origins of this drink. Alexander Woollcott, a drama critic, claimed it was named after him. A New York bartender called Troy Alexander may or may not have created this cocktail. It may have been named for Russian tsar Alexander II, who was Emperor of Russia in the mid-1800s. We do know that John Lennon liked to drink them. It has also been featured in TV shows and movies, including *Two Lovers*, starring Gwyneth Paltrow and Joaquin Phoenix. It is a fairly sweet and rich drink, perhaps best served after dinner. This cocktail is traditionally served up but is also lovely in an old fashioned glass with ice.

INGREDIENTS & METHOD

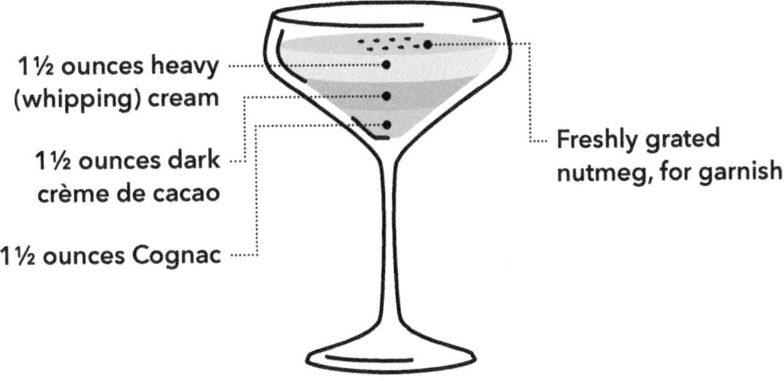

Pour the heavy cream, crème de cacao, and Cognac into the shaker. **Shake** with ice vigorously until very cold, about 15 seconds. **Strain** into the chilled glass. **Grate** the nutmeg on top.

For a lighter version, substitute light cream, half-and-half, or milk for the heavy cream. If using milk, shake the ingredients until very cold, about 15 seconds.

Bellini,
page 116

11

Champagne and Sparkling Wines

The word champagne is often misused to describe all sparkling wines. Although sparkling wine is produced all over the world, true champagne must be produced in the Champagne region of France. Prosecco is a sparkling wine that is a little on the sweet side. It is made in the Veneto region of Italy and is very popular and readily available. Sparkling wine can add a little effervescence to a cocktail and just makes it seem a little extra fancy. Or adding just a few ingredients to a glass of sparkling wine can make something new and festive.

french 75

GLASSWARE & TOOLS

- Champagne flute (chilled)
- Citrus juicer/ extractor
- Jigger
- Shaker
- Hawthorne strainer
- Bar spoon
- Vegetable peeler

Like the Sidecar, this drink is believed to have emerged in the World War I era. Named for the French army's 75 mm field gun, it first appeared in print in the 1927 book *Here's How!*, a Prohibition-era cocktail publication. It has been enjoyed by Queen Victoria's son, the Prince of Wales, and featured in the movie *Casablanca*. If you've tried the Tom Collins, it is more or less the same drink, except here we use sparkling wine instead of club soda and serve it without ice in a champagne flute. It is important for this drink to be very cold, so keep the sparkling wine on ice or in a very cold refrigerator.

INGREDIENTS & METHOD

Fill the shaker halfway with ice and add the simple syrup, lemon juice, and gin. **Shake** until very cold, about 15 seconds. **Strain** into the chilled champagne flute. **Top** with the sparkling wine. **Stir** gently to combine. **Using** the vegetable peeler, make a lemon twist about 2 inches long. **Express** the oils from the peel, rub the twist on the rim, and garnish with the twist.

When expressing the oils from the lemon twist, don't worry if some of the oils get on the outside of the glass. When the drinker picks up the glass, some of those oils will get on their fingers and make the experience even more fragrant. We call this "dressing the glass."

mimosa

GLASSWARE & TOOLS

Champagne flute (chilled)

Citrus juice/ extractor

Bar spoon

The name apparently comes from the yellow flowering mimosa plant, formally known as *acacia dealbata,* which is native to Australia. As with many other drinks, there are several stories about where it was first made. However, it seems to have originated in Spain around the year 1900. The proportions remain debatable. A 1:1 mix is often cited as the official recipe, but that is a bit too juicy for our tastes. Instead, we like a ratio of 4:1 sparkling wine to orange juice, but of course you can adjust to your liking.

INGREDIENTS & METHOD

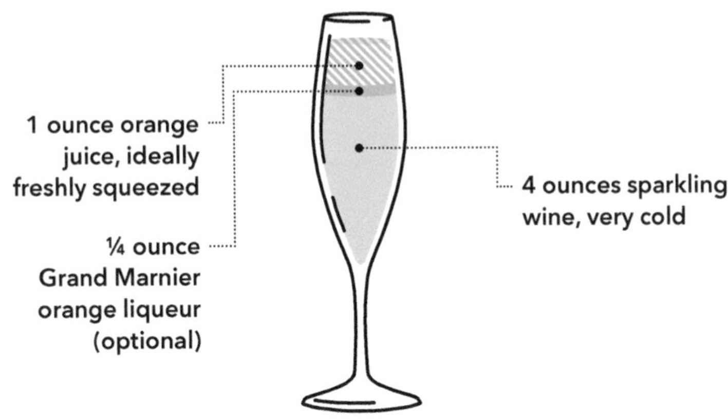

Pour the orange juice and Grand Marnier (if using) into the chilled glass. **Top** with the sparkling wine. **Stir** gently to combine, about three rotations.

TIP No need to spend a lot of money on sparkling wine for this drink. An inexpensive cava (meaning "cave") from Spain works well. Freshly squeezed orange juice transforms this into a very special treat.

bellini

GLASSWARE & TOOLS

Champagne flute (chilled)

Bar spoon

The Bellini was first made by Giuseppe Cipriani, proprietor of Harry's Bar in Venice, Italy. It was named for the fifteenth-century Venetian artist Giovanni Bellini. Similar to the Mimosa, this drink is a combination of fruit and sparkling wine. In this case the fruit is peach purée, which you may be able to find in the frozen section of your supermarket, or with a little effort you can make your own.

INGREDIENTS & METHOD

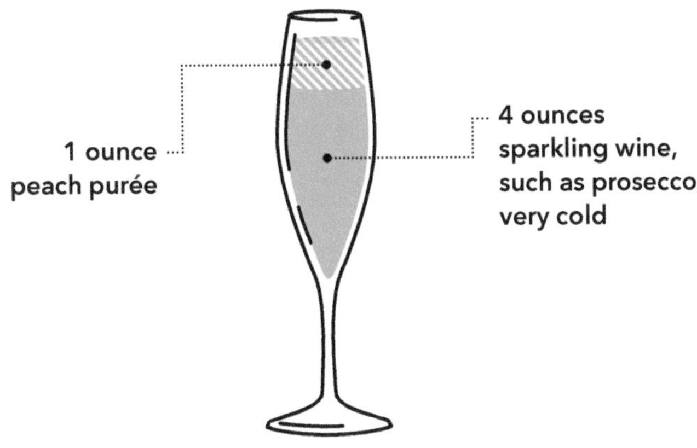

Pour the peach purée into the glass. **Top** with the sparkling wine. **Stir** gently to combine, about three rotations.

TIP

To make your own peach purée, cook two ripe peaches, seeded and diced, with 1 tablespoon of sugar and ½ cup of water over low heat for about 3 minutes, until soft. Purée in a food processor or blender. You can also purée some canned peaches—we won't tell.

kir royale

GLASSWARE & TOOLS

Champagne flute (chilled)

Bar spoon

This drink is derived from the Kir cocktail, which is still (nonsparkling) white wine and crème de cassis, a liqueur made from black currants. Using sparkling wine, such as French champagne, rather than still wine produces the fancy Kir Royale cocktail. This drink is beautiful and festive. It is great for brunch or before dinner with hors d'oeuvres. Crème de cassis can be a little difficult to source; a well-stocked liquor store will have it, but substituting the more widely available Chambord, made with raspberries, is not such a bad thing.

INGREDIENTS & METHOD

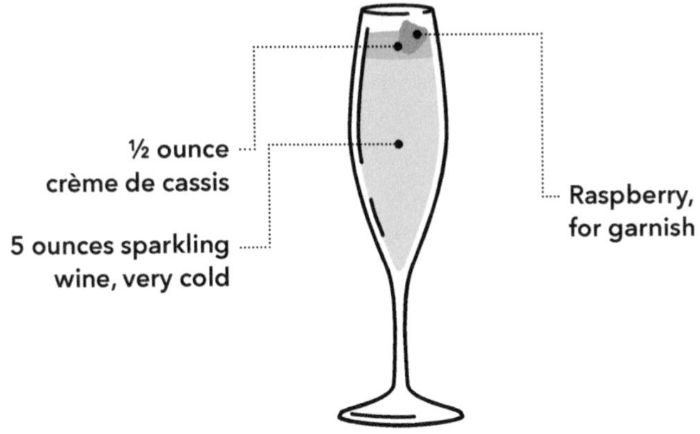

Pour the crème de cassis into the glass. **Top** with the sparkling wine. **Stir** gently to combine, about three rotations. **Drop** a raspberry into the glass.

champagne cocktail

GLASSWARE & TOOLS

Champagne flute (chilled)

Bar spoon

This drink appears in Jerry Thomas's 1862 book *The Bar-tender's Guide: How to Mix Drinks, or The Bon-Vivant's Companion.* "Professor" Jerry Thomas's version did not include brandy, but some later recipes did call for it. It's optional in our opinion. Jerry Thomas's version also called for "broken" ice. However, it is now traditionally served without ice in a champagne flute. The sugar cube goes into the glass and dissolves as it is being consumed, causing an interesting and festive visual effect.

INGREDIENTS & METHOD

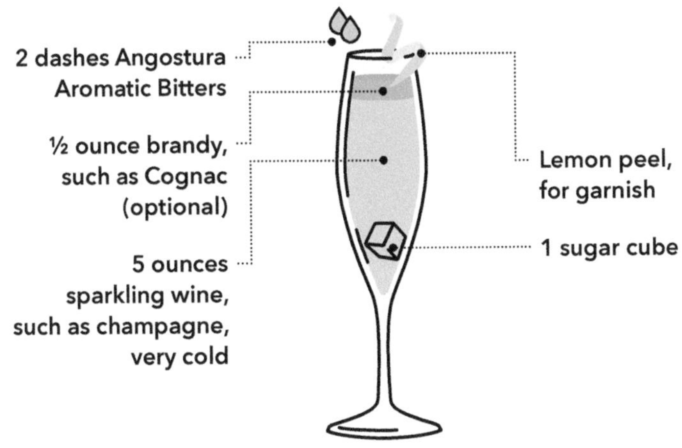

Place the sugar cube on a plate or another surface. **Soak** it with the Angostura Aromatic Bitters. **Put** the sugar cube in the champagne flute. **Add** the brandy (if using). **Top** with the sparkling wine. **Garnish** with the lemon peel.

Aperol Spritz,
page 124

12

Liqueurs and Apéritifs

For most cocktails, liqueurs play a supporting role; although more flavorful than other liquid ingredients, they are usually low ABV (alcohol by volume), and as a secondary ingredient to a base spirit they aren't able to shine with their natural flavors. However, cocktails have evolved to complement cultural trends, such as the invention of brunch and the recent health movement highlighting drinks with lower alcohol content, less sugar, and citrusy flavors. Liqueurs now shine as natural headliners of light and refreshing cocktails that are perfect for day drinking. As a prelude to heavier meals, such as dinner, apéritifs have been lauded as aiding with digestion.

aperol spritz

GLASSWARE & TOOLS

- Large wine glass
- Jigger
- Bar spoon

The Aperol Spritz is a low-ABV drink that is a bit citrusy, bubbly, and a little bitter. It is usually served in a wine glass with an orange slice. Aperol Spritzes have long been popular in Europe and have been creating quite a stir in the United States in recent years. Its inviting red-orange color and refreshing taste appeals to many people, especially since it's easy to make and fun to share.

INGREDIENTS & METHOD

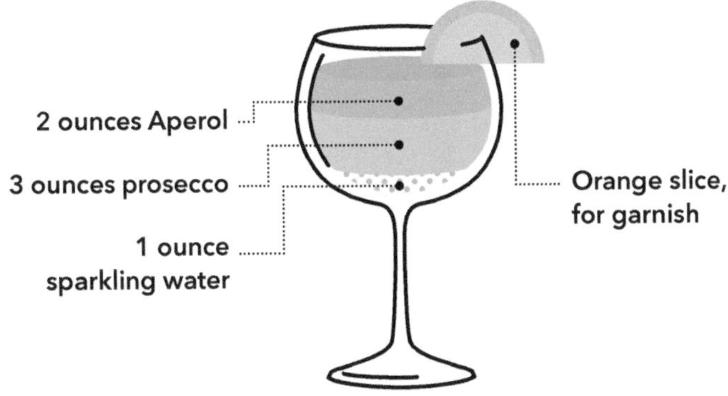

Fill the wine glass about halfway with ice. **Add** the Aperol, then the prosecco and sparkling water. **Stir** gently with the bar spoon to combine, about three rotations. **Add** the orange slice to the glass.

Aperol is a bitter Italian apéritif that dates back to 1919. It comprises "an infusion of selected herbs and roots." While tastemakers agree that gentian, rhubarb, and orange are some of the primary flavors, the full recipe remains a secret.

pimm's cup

GLASSWARE & TOOLS

- Collins glass
- Jigger
- Shaker
- Muddler
- Bar spoon
- Hawthorne strainer
- Mesh strainer (optional but recommended)

About 40,000 British versions of this cocktail are sold annually at Wimbledon. It's made with Pimm's No. 1, originally sold as a health tonic by James Pimm in the 1840s. No one knows exactly what is in Pimm's No. 1, and the recipe remains a closely guarded secret to this day. As a cocktail, Pimm's No. 1 was served in tankards, i.e., tall beer mugs, which accounts for the "cup" part of the name. Stateside, the US version is rumored to have been created in the Napoleon House bar by a bar owner looking for a refreshing low-alcohol option for his patrons to enjoy all night long in the New Orleans heat.

INGREDIENTS & METHOD

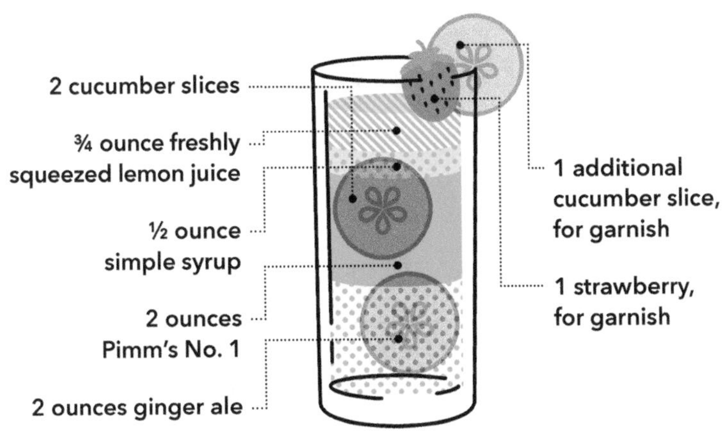

Muddle the two cucumber slices in the shaker and then add the lemon juice, simple syrup, and Pimm's No 1. **Add** ice and shake until very cold, about 15 seconds. **Double** strain into the glass and add the ginger ale and desired amount of ice. **Garnish** with the cucumber slice and strawberry.

sloe gin fizz

GLASSWARE & TOOLS

- Collins glass
- Jigger
- Shaker
- Hawthorne strainer

Sloe gin is not a type of gin but rather a red liqueur from steeping with sugar, gin, and sloe berries, native to England. Sloe berries themselves grew out of a seventeenth-century land act that required hedgerows to mark individual properties. Enterprising Brits decided to offset the tart taste of the berries with gin, and thus sloe gin or the "poor man's port" was born. With the recent craft cocktail revival, bartenders began incorporating it into the summertime drink and brunch culture.

INGREDIENTS & METHOD

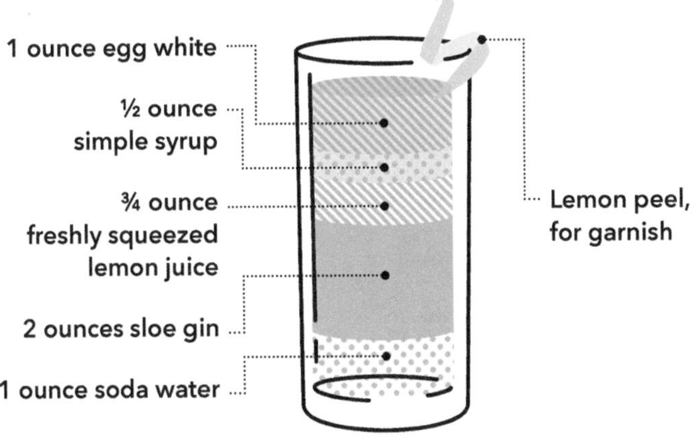

Pour the egg white, simple syrup, lemon juice, and sloe gin into the shaker. **Add** ice and shake until chilled, about 15 seconds. **Strain** out the ice and give it a double shake. **Pour** the mixed cocktail into the glass and then add the soda and fresh ice. **Express** the oils from the peel over the finished cocktail and rest it on top.

If you prefer not to use an egg white for this recipe, double the soda water to 2 ounces.

amaretto sour

GLASSWARE & TOOLS

- Collins glass, rocks glass, or old fashioned glass
- Jigger
- Shaker
- Hawthorne strainer

In 1969, Mario Puzo's novel *The Godfather* was published, followed by the movie version a few years later. The commercial success of the book and film launched an Italian pride movement among restaurant and bar owners, who then chose to emphasize their Italian origins wherever possible. Italian spirits and liqueurs in the United States were the '70s rage, and amaretto di Saronno was introduced stateside, also marketed as Disaronno. It's a popular theory that the Amaretto Sour was naturally created to meet public demand for Italian cocktails. Either way, it's a tasty sour cocktail that you're sure to enjoy.

INGREDIENTS & METHOD

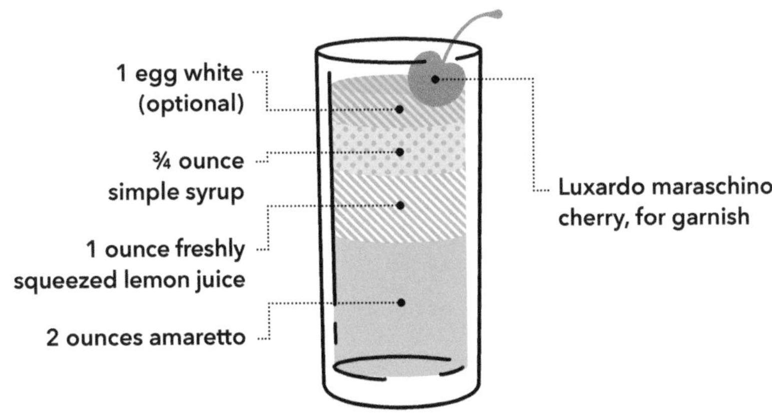

Pour the egg white (if using), simple syrup, lemon juice, and amaretto into the shaker. **Add** ice and shake until very cold, about 15 seconds. **If** using the egg white, strain out the ice and use the double shake method. **Pour** the mixed cocktail into the glass filled with fresh ice. **Garnish** with the Luxardo maraschino cherry.

americano

GLASSWARE & TOOLS

Collins glass

Jigger

Bar spoon

This classic cocktail was originally known as the Milano-Torino, named after the geographical origin of its two main ingredients: Campari (Milan) and Italian vermouth (Torino). It was created by Gaspare Campari and served in a bar in the 1860s. It was rumored to be renamed the Americano either after the Italian boxer Primo Carnera, who fought in the United States, or due to the fact that Italians witnessed a significant number of Americans enjoying it in Italy. A fun trivia fact is that its literary debut was as James Bond's first drink of choice in the *Casino Royale* novel by Ian Fleming.

INGREDIENTS & METHOD

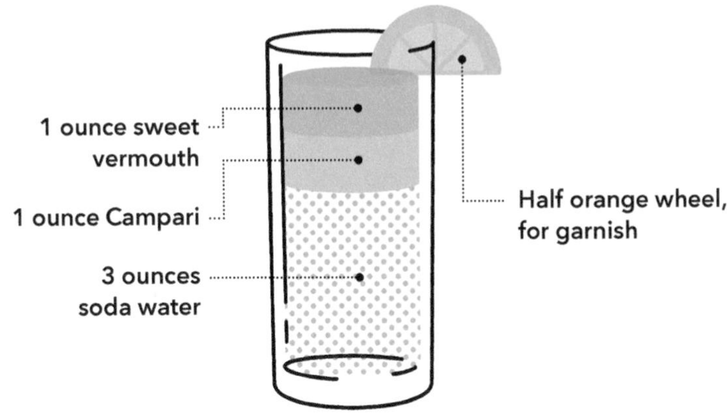

Pour the sweet vermouth, Campari, and soda into the glass. **Add** ice and stir gently to combine, about three rotations. **Garnish** with a half orange wheel.

“

A COCKTAIL DONE RIGHT CAN REALLY SHOW YOUR GUESTS THAT YOU CARE.

—**Danny Meyer**

measurements and conversion table

VOLUME EQUIVALENTS (LIQUID)

US STANDARD	US STANDARD (OUNCES)	METRIC (APPROXIMATE)
2 tablespoons	1 fl. oz.	30 mL
¼ cup	2 fl. oz.	60 mL
½ cup	4 fl. oz.	120 mL
1 cup	8 fl. oz.	240 mL
1½ cups	12 fl. oz.	355 mL
2 cups or 1 pint	16 fl. oz.	475 mL
4 cups or 1 quart	32 fl. oz.	1 L
1 gallon	128 fl. oz.	4 L

resources

books

- *The Bar Book: Elements of Cocktail Technique* by Jeffrey Morgenthaler
- *The Craft of the Cocktail: Everything You Need to Know to Be a Master Bartender* by Dale DeGroff
- *The Joy of Mixology: The Consummate Guide to the Bartender's Craft* by Gary Regan
- *Regarding Cocktails* by Sasha Petraske
- *Smuggler's Cove: Exotic Cocktails, Rum, and the Cult of Tiki* by Martin Cate and Rebecca Cate

websites

- BeautifulBooze.com
- GoodSpiritsNews.wordpress.com
- ImbibeMagazine.com
- PunchDrink.com
- ThirstyMag.com

index

N

O

P

R

S

acknowledgments

We'd like to thank everyone who helped us on our own Bartender Journeys. We can't list everyone here, but special thanks to:

BRIAN The guests and audience of my podcast, *Bartender Journey*. Gary "Gaz" Regan and Dale DeGroff for the education and inspiration. Tales of the Cocktail, Bar Institute, Bar Methods, and the United States Bartenders' Guild for learning opportunities and community connection. Finally, thanks to Hazel Alvarado for your ongoing encouragement, advocacy, and invaluable contributions to both this book and the podcast.

BENNY I would like to praise my wife, Nichole, and daughter, Simone, who have always supported me. Thanks to the people, brands, and resorts that helped create my career. I applaud the hard work of Brian Weber and Hazel Alvarado. Without the hard work of everyone within the United States Bartenders' Guild, this cocktail culture and community would not be where we are. I would not have been able to write this book without my teachers in the industry, who authored books and educated the community.

about the authors

BRIAN WEBER Beginning at age 14, Brian washed dishes for $15 a night. He worked as a line cook, server, bartender, manager, and eventually head chef of a Manhattan restaurant by 23. He later worked at a New York City recording studio that was shuttered by the 2008 financial crisis. Brian pivoted by launching an audio production business while also professionally bartending full time at a private club. In 2013, Brian merged his passions, bartending and audio production, creating the educational podcast *Bartender Journey*. He has been featured as a panelist at the industry conference Tales of the Cocktail ("Podcasting for Bartenders") and as an industry expert on Crafty Bartending ("Industry Pros Give Advice for New Bartenders") and Meet the People ("5 Podcasts Every Bartender Should Be Listening To"). Brian continues to bartend near his home in Monroe, New York, and work on both audio production projects and cocktail consulting projects.

AMIN BENNY Amin Benny is a veteran bartender who has created cocktails at some of the top resorts on the West Coast while serving as founder and president of the Orange County chapter of the United States Bartenders' Guild (USBG). He created his own bar consulting business called The Bar Host; he is also Steward of the Brand for WhistlePig Rye Whiskey. After a long bartending career in Las Vegas, Nevada, Benny currently lives in Orange County, California, with his lovely wife Nichole and amazing daughter Simone. Educated by some of the top mixologists in the United States, Benny is driven by his desire to share his knowledge with developing bartenders and cocktail enthusiasts alike.

CPSIA information can be obtained
at www.ICGtesting.com
Printed in the USA
LVHW072018171019
634283LV00003B/3/P